Middlesex County, Virginia

Court Order Book
(May 1783–April 1784)

and

Land Records
(October 1785–1790)

Richard S. Hutchinson

HERITAGE BOOKS
2020

HERITAGE BOOKS

AN IMPRINT OF HERITAGE BOOKS, INC.

Books, CDs, and more—Worldwide

For our listing of thousands of titles see our website
at
www.HeritageBooks.com

Published 2020 by
HERITAGE BOOKS, INC.
Publishing Division
5810 Ruatan Street
Berwyn Heights, Md. 20740

International Standard Book Number
Paperbound: 978-1-68034-486-8

CONTENTS

iv

INTRODUCTION

Middlesex County, Virginia
Court Order book
May 1783 – April 1784

This book includes various Court cases, appointments, names of deceased residents, many named Slaves with some owners who registered them as "set free of County Levy," County officials being paid in pounds of tobacco for their official duties, and several references to the Revolutionary War effort wherein individuals listed the items or services rendered for the cause.

Middlesex County, Virginia
Land Records
Oct 1785 – 1790

The dates of these documents have a few items dated earlier than 1785 and also have a couple other dated in 1791.

The information found in these documents includes various family relationships, some prenuptial agreements, the approximate dates of deaths, the names of hundreds of Slaves and their owners, who bought, sold, gifted, or put them up for collateral for land, and used them to pay off the owner's previous debts. Also the main agricultural crop was tobacco which was used in barter and payment for salaries of officials and purchase of land. If you are looking for dates of birth, date, etc. for those in the Parish of Christ Church, Middlesex, County, Virginia, including the vital statistics of the Slaves, search the Register of the Parish, which was published but can also be found online at the LDS website.

William Churchill was the County Clerk for Middlesex County, Virginia. The person copying these documents consistently spelled the name as "CHURCHHILL" in the book. I have spelled the named as "CHURCHILL" in this book.

ABBREVIATIONS

a. - acre, acres
absd. – abovesaid
abt. – about
ackn. – acknowledge
adj. – adjoining
Admin. – administration, administrator, administratrix
afsd.- aforesaid
apprd. – appeared
atty. – attorney, attorneys
bef. – before
beg. – begins, beginning
betw. – between
bnd. – bound, bounds
bot. – bought
Co. – county
crk. – creek
d. – died, dead
dau. – daughter
daus. – daughters
dec'd. – deceased
e. – east
Esqr. – Esquire
exec. – executor, executors, executrix
excep. – except, excepting
[FNU] – First Name Unknown
form. – formerly
Gent. – gentleman
[LNU] – Last Name Unknown
n. – north
pt. – part
pt/o. – part of
recr'd. – record, recorded
s. – south
sd. – said
tr. – tract, tracts
Twp. – township
w. – west
wch. – which
wits. – witness, witnesses
w/o. - without

Middlesex Co., Virginia Court Order Book

May 1783 – April 1784

Page 1.

At a Court held for Middlesex Co. at the Court House in Urbanna on Monday the 26th day of May 1783

Present – Philip Mountague, Overton Cosby, Henry Vass, James Ross, Gent.

Ordered that Mary Blackburn's list of Taxable Property to be added to the general list.

Ordered that Daniel Dejarnett's list of Taxable Property to be added to the general list.

Letters of Administration on the Estate of William Brooks is granted to Thomas Brooks, he having taken the Oath of the Administrator, and entered into Bond with John Healy, his Security in the penalty of £300 with conditions according to law.

Present -Thomas Segar, Gent.

Ordered that Thomas Healy, Robert Stamper, Nicholas Tuggle & James Kidd or any three of them being first sworn bef. some Justice of the Peace for this County do appraise the Estate of William Brooks deceased and their report to next Court.

Ordered that Robert Thurston's Chair [?] to be added in the general list of Taxable property.

Settlement of the Estate of John Tuggle, dec'd, returned and Ordered to be recorded.

Robert Thurston is appointed by the Court Guardian of John Chowning, Orphan of John Chowning, he having entered into Bond with Daniel Dejarnett in the penalty sum of £100 with conditions according to law.

Simon Laughlin's Negroe Daphny & Daniel are set County Levee free.

Daniel Dejanatt's Negroe Sarah is Set County Levy free.

2

Absent - Overton Cosby, Gent.

Administration amount of the estate of Robert Wake returned and ordered to be recorded.

In Debt - James Lee, Pltf, VS Simon Laughlen, Deft. For reasons appearing to the Court the suit is dismissed.

Nelson Daniel, foreman; John Jackson, Junr.; Daniel Dejarnatt; Simon Laughlin; John Morgan; George Sanders; John Clark; Benjamin Kidd; Harry Beverley Yates; Henry Batchelder; John Dunlevy; William Hackney; Benjamin Swords; Nicholas Tuggle; William Jones; and Thomas Patterson were sworn a Grand Jury of Inquest for the Body of this County, and having received their Charge retired from the Bar to consult of their verdict, and after some time returned into Court and made the following Presentments. to wit. – Ann Dudley for a bastard Child; Thomas Edwards for getting Drunk and swearing one Oath the 22 of April; Charles Grymes for swearing four Oaths the 22nd of April; John Wake, Senr., for concealing the whole of his Taxable property; Robert Wake for ditto; John Paush[?] for ditto; Josiah Poush[?] ditto; Dudley Vann for ditto; John Sole for concealing [can't read]; Edward Brooks for Ditto; Mary Dor_____ ? concealing her Taxable Property; Susanna Daniels

Page 2 [?].

For not keeping his Mill Bridge in repair, the Surveyor of the Road from William Elliot's Mill to the peping[?] trees. Henry Linn for concealing his Taxable property. John Humphries for concealing his Taxable property. Sarah Hugging for bastard child and then the Grand Jury having nothing for her to present was discharged.

Ordered that the several persons presented by the Grand Jury be summoned to appear at and Court.

Ordered that Edward Didlake list of Taxable property be added to the general list.

John Jackson, Junr. is appointed Surveyor of the highways in the room of John Swords.

John George, Junr. is allowed to keep an Ordinary in the County he having entered into Bond with Security according to Law.

Benjamin Kidd is permitted to keep an Ordinary in the County he having entered into Bond with Security according to Law.

James Kidd is permitted to keep an Ordinary in the County he having entered into Bond with Security according to Law.

James Piggot is appointed Survey of the highway in the room of Thomas Healy.

Absent James Ross, Gent. Present George Daniel, Gent.

In Debt - John Hughes assignee of William Clayton, Exec. of John Clayton – Pltf. VS John Robinson, Exec. of Augustine Curtis – Deft. Came as well the Pltf. by Benjamin Dabney his attorney as the Deft. by George Lyne his attorney and the sd. Deft. prays and has leave to Imparle here till She meat and then to plead.

In Debt - Edward Spencer Admin. of Thomas Spencer Pltf. VS Robert Thurston Deft. The Deft. not being arrested on the motion of the Pltf. by his attorney on Alias Capias is awarded him against the sd. Deft. returnable here at the next Court.

In Debt - Robert Green assigner of Thomas Withie[?] Plft. VS William Elliot Deft. The sd. Deft. not being arrested on the motion of the sd. Pltf. by his attorney on Alias Capias is awarded him against the sd. Deft. returnable here at the next Court.

In Debt - John Humphries VS Elizabeth Hackney & William Hackney Defts. This suit in continued till next Court.

Page 3 [?]

Joseph Hardee the sd. Deft. not being arrested on the motion of the sd. Pltf. by his attorney on Alias Capias is awarded him against the sd. Deft. returnable here at the next Court.

In Case – John Montague VS George Lorimer Exec. of Mary Elizabeth Thacker Deft. by order of the Pltf. this Suit is dismissed.

In Debt – William Dudley & Henry Fleet, Exec. of Edwin Fleet Exec. of William Fleet Pltf. VS William Gest Deft. The sd. Deft. not being arrested on the motion of the sd. Pltf. by his attorney on Alias Capias is awarded them against the sd. Deft. returnable here at the next Court.

In Debt - William Dudley & Henry Fleet Exec. of Edwin Fleet assignee of Aggy Holderby Pltf. VS William Gest . The sd. Deft. not being arrested on the motion of the sd. Pltf. by their attorney on Alias Capias is awarded them against the sd. Deft. returnable here at the next Court.

In Case - John Throckmorton Pltf. VA Lawrence Meacham Deft. came the Plft. by his attorney and the sd. Deft. by his attorney whereupon William Churchill came into Court and undertakes the Deft. that if he shall be cast in this Action that he the sd. Deft. shall pay the Costs and Condemnation of the Court, or render his body to Prison in discharge thereof or that he the sd. William Churchill will pay the Costs and Condemnation for him, and therefore the sd. Deft. prays and has leave to Imparle here till the next Court and then to plead.

On Repleasy [?] Bond – James Mills & Co. Pltf. VS William Armistead Deft. On the motion of the sd. Pltf. against William Armistead Deft. he having had ten days previous notice, Execution is awarded the sd. Pltf. against the sd. Deft. for £116,8 shillings, and one penny and the costs of the Motion. But the Judgment to be discharged by the payment of £58, 4 shillings and a half-penny with interest at the rate of five per centum per annum to be computed from the third day of March 1764 to the time of payment and the costs.

Present - Overton Cosby & William Munay[Murray?] Gent.

In case - George Green Pltf. VS John Curtis Deft. [bottom of page missing].

Page 4.

[can't read] ….he the sd. Deft. shall pay the costs and Condemnation of the Court, or order his Body to Prison in Discharge thereof, or that the sd. Thomas [can't read] pay the costs & Condemnation, for him, therefore the sd. Deft. prays and has leave to Imparle separately here till the [?] Court and then to plead.

In Chancery - Alexander Anderson & Nanny, his wife, Thomas Scott, John Scott, Esther Scott, & Elizabeth Scott, Pltf. VS Nancy Scott and Infant & Sally Scott, her Guardian, Defts. This Suit is continued till next Court for Bill.

In Debt - George Lorimer, Pltf. VS John Montague, Exec. of James Montague, dec'd, Deft. came the Pltf. by his attorney and the Deft. by his attorney and the sd. Deft. prays and has leave here to Imparle till next Court and then to Plead.

John Layton, Pltf., VS George Pasquet, Deft. came the Pltf. by his attorney and the Deft. by his attorney and the sd. Deft. prays and has leave here to Imparle till next Court and then to Plead.

On Sec Facias – William Clayton, Exec. of Augustine Smith, dec'd, Deft., This Suit abates by return.

Absent - George Daniel, Gent.

On Petition - George & Beverley Daniel, Exec. of Robert Daniel, dec'd, Admin of John Aldin, dec'd, Pltf. VS Benjamin Williamson, Deft. This Petition is continued till next Court.

Absent - Philip Mountague. Present James Ross, Gent.

In Case - James Gregorie & George Lorimer, Exec. of John Daniel, dec'd, Pltf. VS Samuel Chowning, Deft. This Suit is continued till next Court.

In Case - William Montague, Pltf. VS Samuel Chowning, Deft. This Suit is continued till next Court.

In Case - Philip Edwards Jones, Pltf. VS Isaac Jones, Deft. This Suit is continued till next Court.

Page 5.

In Case - Edmund Pendleton & Peter Lyons, Admins. of John Robinson, dec'd, Pltf. VS Christopher Robinson, Deft. The sd. Deft. not being arrested on the motion of the Pltf. by their attorney an Alias [can't read] Capias is awarded them against the sd. Deft. returnable here at the next Court.

In Chancery - Christopher Curtis & wife, Pltf. VS William Murray, Deft. This suit abates.

William Bristow's Negroe Frank is set County Levy free.

Philip Ludwell Grymes' Negroe Harry is set County Levy free.

Thomas Patterson's Negroe Simon is set County Levy free.

William Churchill's Negroe Cassius is set County Levy free.

In Case – John Quarles, Pltf. VS John Pendleton, Admin., of William Parry, Deft. This Suit abates the Pltf. Death.

In Chancery - Thomas Iveson & others, Pltf. VS Jane, Sally & Elizabeth Morgan, etc, Deft. This Suit is continued for report.

Robert Thurston's Negroe Rachel is set County Levy free.

In Chancery - Simon Laughlin, Pltf., VS Robert Massey, Deft. This Suit is continued till next Court. This Suit abates the Pltf. death.

6

In Chancery - Simon Laughlin, Pltf., VS Ann Tomkins, Deft. This Suit is continued till next Court.

In Case - Joseph Hardee, Pltf. VS Charles Neilson, Deft. This Suit abates the Deft's. death.

Joseph Gayle & wife, Pltf. VS Isaac Jones, Deft. This Suit abates the Deft's. death.

Page 6.

[Can't read first two lines]

The Suit in Chancery depending betw. William Montague as Pltf. and James & Mary Ritchie, Deft. in continued till next court.

The Suit in Chancery depending betw. Paulin Anderson & others and William Churchill and others is continued till next court.

Settlement of William Roane's Administration of John Murray's Estate continued.

The Suit in Chancery depending betw. William Churchill, Pltf., and Frances Williams[?], Deft., attachment with Proclamation is awarded the Pltf.

The Suit in Chancery depending betw. Carter Braxton, Pltf., and the of Christopher Robinson is continued till next Court.

The Suit in Chancery depending betw. Roger Blackburn, Pltf., and William Blackburn, Deft. is abated by the Deft.'s death.

The Suit in Chancery depending betw. William Jones, Pltf., and George Sanders[?], Deft., is continued till next Court.

The Suit in Chancery depending betw. Gibson Jones, Pltf., and John Blake, Deft., is continued till next Court.

Settlement of John Berry's Estate continued.

The Suit in Chancery depending betw. William Churchill, Pltf.., and Thomas and George Sanders, Deft., is continued till next Court.

The Suit in Chancery depending betw. William Montague as Pltf., and Charles Neilson and others, Deft., abate as to Charles Neilson by his death & continued till next Court against the others.

The Suit in Chancery depending betw. William Clayton, of John Clayton, Pltf., and Augustine Smith, Philip Ludwell Grymes, Warner Lewis, William Churchill and Churchill Jones, Deft., abates as to Smith and continued till next Court against the others.

The Attachment brought by John & George Fowlers, Pltf., and John Adair, Deft., is continued till next Court.

A Deed from William Thurston and Rebecca, his wife, with the receipt thereon, endorsed to Harry Beverley Yates was proved by the Oaths of the Witnesses thereto wch. together with a Commission for the privy examination of the sd. Rebecca returned and is Ordered to be Recorded.

Absent - George Daniel, Gent.

In Case - George Bird VS of Hannah Price[?], Deft. [Can't read the bottom line of this case]

Page 7

[Can't read the first line but possible a re-write of the last item on Page 6.]

Henry Vass, Gent., is appointed to take the list of tithes for the upper precinct in this County. Thomas Roane, Gent., in the Middle Precinct and James Ross, Gent., is the town precinct.

Ordered that George Daniel, Overton Cosby, & James Ross, Gent, or any two of them to examine the Clerk's Office and make their report to next Court.

Ordered that the Court be adjourned to the Court in Course. The Minutes of these proceedings were signed by Philip Mountague, Gent.

At a Court held for Middlesex County at the Court House in Urbanna on Monday the 23d day of June 1783

Present - Philip Mountague, Henry Vass, George Daniel, James Ross, Gent.

Presentment of the Grand Jury - Commonwealth, Pltf., VS Mary Dudley, Deft., for reasons appearing to the Court this Suit is dismissed.

Ordered that Mary Dudley's list of Taxable property be added to the general list.

Presentment of the Grand Jury - Commonwealth VS Joseph Parish, Deft.

for reasons appearing to the Court this Suit is dismissed.

The last Will and Testament of Henry Mickelburrough, dec'd, was presented to the Court by Henry Street, one of the Execs. therein named, who made Oath according to Law and the same was proved by the Oaths of Charles Curtis and Thomas Willis, two of the Witnesses thereto and Ordered to be Recorded. And, on the motion of the sd. Certificate is granted him for blaming a Probation due from giving Security, whereon he had with George Bird, his Security, entered into and ackn.d their Bond in the penalty of £3,000 with Condition according to Law. (lease is granted to the Execs to qualify.)

Ordered that Thomas Healy, James Kidd, Robert Stamper and Lawrence Meacham or any three of them being first sworn bef. same Justice of the Peace for this County do appear the Estate of Henry Mickelburrough, dec'd, and make their to the next Court.

Presentment of the Grand Jury - Commonwealth, Pltf., VS John Sole, Deft., for reasons appearing to the Court this Suit is dismissed.

Letters of Administration is granted to Sarah Bayton on the Estate of William Bayton [can't read the rest].

Page 8

{Order on the Estate of William Bayton – can't read the rest of item].

Appraisement of the Estate of William Brooks returned & ordered to be continued.

Presentment of the Grand Jury - Commonwealth, Pltf., VS Dudley Vaughan, Deft. for reasons appearing to the Court this Suit is dismissed.

Ordered that George Bird, Philip Mountague and Thomas Segar, Gent., or any two of them, do advertise for the building of the old Mill Bridge and let the same to the lowest bidder to be kept in repair for seven years and that they take Bond with Security for the performance of the same.

Absent - George Daniel, present William Murray, Gent.

Presentment of the Grand Jury - Commonwealth, Pltf., VS Henry Lynn, Deft., for reasons appearing to the Court this Suit is dismissed.

Ordered that the list of Taxable property belonging to Henry Lynn, Dudley Vaughan, John Parish and John Humphries, Junr, be added to the general list.

Presentment of the Grand Jury - Commonwealth, Pltf., VS John Parish, Deft., for reasons appearing to the Court this Suit is dismissed.

Presentment of the Grand Jury - Commonwealth, Pltf., VS John Humphries, Junr., Deft., for reasons appearing to the Court this Suit is dismissed.

Absent - James Ross, present Thomas Segar, Gent.

George Bird, Henry Vass, and Thomas Segar, Gent. are recommended to his Excellency Benjamin Harrison, Esqr., Gov. as proper persons to be accepted to the office of Sheriff for this County.

Presentment of the Grand Jury - Commonwealth, Pltf., VS Sarah Hudgin, Deft., for reasons appearing to the Court this Suit is Continued till next Court.

Absent - Thomas Segar, present Overton Cosby, Gent.

Presentment of the Grand Jury - Commonwealth, Pltf., VS Susanna Daniel, Deft., for reasons appearing to the Court this Suit is dismissed.

Page 9

Presentment of the Grand Jury - Commonwealth, Pltf., VS Jacob Stiff Saunders., Deft., for reasons appearing to the Court this Suit is dismissed.

Presentment of the Grand Jury - Commonwealth, Pltf., VS Edward Brooks., Deft., the said Deft. not being arrested on the motion of the sd. Pltf. by its attorney on alias Capias is awarded against the sd. Deft. returnable here at the next Court.

Presentment of the Grand Jury - Commonwealth, Pltf., VS Robert Wake., Deft., This day came the Pltf., by Thomas Moore its attorney and the Deft. not appearing it is considered by the Court that the sd. Offence he make his fine to the Commonwealth by the payment of 500 [lbs.] of tobacco and the costs.

Presentment of the Grand Jury - Commonwealth, Pltf., VS John Wake., Deft., not appearing it is considered by the Court that the sd. Offence he make his fine to the Commonwealth by the payment of _____ [lbs.] of tobacco and the costs.

Present - George Daniel, absent Philip Mountague, Gent.

Presentment of the Grand Jury - Commonwealth, Pltf., VS Charles Grymes., Deft., not appearing it is considered by the Court that the sd. Offence he make his fine to the Commonwealth by the payment of one pound of tobacco and the costs.

Presentment of the Grand Jury - Commonwealth, Pltf., VS Ann Dudley., Deft., for reasons appearing to the Court this Suit is continued till next Court.

In Case - James Lee, Pltf., VS Simon Laughlin, Deft., came the Pltf. by his attorney and the Deft. by his attorney and the sd. Deft. prays and has leave to Imparle here and plead at the next Court.

In Case - John Mountague, Pltf., VS George Lorimer, of Mary Elizabeth Thacker, Deft., came the Pltf. by his attorney and the Deft. his attorney and the sd. Deft. prays and has leave to Imparle here and plead at the next Court.

In Case - Francis Stubbs, Pltf. VS John Layton, Deft.

Page 10

[appears to be continued from the previous page]The sd. Deft. being [can't read] the motion of the sd. Pltf. by his attorney on attachment is [can't read] him for £15 and costs of the suit against the Estate of the sd. Deft. & returnable to the next Court.

In Case - Mary Mercer, Admin., of Isaac Mercer, dec'd, Pltf. VS George Lorimer, Came the Pltf. by his attorney and the sd. Deft. by his attorney and the Deft. prays & has leave to Imparle here and plea at the next Court.

In Case – John George, Junr., Pltf. VS Griffin Tuggle, Deft. Came the Pltf. by his attorney, and the sd. Deft. by his attorney where upon Robert Thurston comes into Court and undertakes for the Deft., that if he should be cast in this action that he, the sd. Deft., shall pay the costs and condemnation of the Court or render his body to Prison in discharge thereof, or that he the sd. Robert Thurston will pay the costs and condemnation for him, therefore the sd. Deft. prays and have leave of a Plea Oyer his till next Court and then to plea.

Absent - Henry Vass, Gent.

In Debt - William Goosley, Pltf., VS Charles Grymes, Deft., by order of the Pltf., this suit is dismissed.

In Petition - Benjamin Dabney, Pltf., VS John Sole, Deft., for reasons appearing to the Court this Suit is continued till next Court.

Present - Philip Mountague, Gent.

Matthias James, Pltf. VS George Jackson, Deft., by order of the Pltf. this suit is dismissed the Deft. to pay the costs.

A Claim of William George against the State of Virginia

Same for one day Service as Clerk of the Court for appointing Commissioners for collecting the Clothing & eight days as receiver to the eight division, also for one days service & five days for making and Instructions for the divisions.

Ordered that the Court be adjourned to the Court in Course.

The minutes of these proceedings were signed by Philip Mountague, Gent.

Page 11

At a Court held for Middlesex County at the Courthouse in Urbanna, on Monday the 28th day of July 1784[3?]. Present – Maurice Smith, Philip Mountague, George Daniel, Henry Vass, Overton Cosby, James Ross, Gent.

The Court have appointed according to Law, Philip Mountague & Robert Daniel, Gent., Commissioners for the Land Tax in this County, the sd. Commissioners having taken the Oath prescribed by Law.

The Appraisement of the Estate of Edward Bristow, dec'd, returned & ordered to be amended.

The Last Will & Testament of Sarah Crisp, dec'd, was this day presented in Court by George Lee Turberville, one of the Execs., therein named, who made Oath according to Law and the same was proved by the Oath of Edward Ware, one of the witnesses thereto, and Ordered to be recorded and on the motion of the, Certificate was granted him for obtaining a Probate in due form, giving Security, whereupon he with William Churchill, his security, entered into and ackn.d their Bond in the penalty of £500 with Condition according to Law.

Ordered that the Vestry of Christ Church Parish do appoint processions according to Law.

Absent - Philip Mountague, Gent.

Ordered that Robert Spratt and James Ross, Gent., be added to the former Order of this Court for selling the [ditto] Admin Account of the Estate of John Murray, dec'd.

Presentment of the Grand Jury – The Commonwealth, Pltf., VS Samuel Brooks, Deft., for reasons appearing to the Court this Suit is continued till next Court.

Absent - George Daniel, Gent.

In the motion of James Wortham against Nelson Daniel Judgment is awarded the sd. James for 3,152 lbs Tobacco agreeable to the [can't read] of the Seale in April 1780 & costs.

Present - Philip Mountague and George Daniel, Gent.

By Petition - Benjamin Dabney, Pltf. VS John Soles, Deft, on the motion of the sd. Pltf., this suit is dismissed of the Deft. costs.

Ordered that Dinah and Nelson belonging to Thomas Roane be set County levy free.

Ordered that Tom & Sarah belonging to Benjamin Bristow by set County levy free.

Ordered that this Court be adjourned to the Court in Course. The minutes of these proceedings were signed by Maurice Smith, Gent.

Page 12

At a Court held for Middlesex County at the Courthouse n Urbanna on Monday, the 22nd day of September 1783.

Present – George Daniel, John Daniel, James Ross and William Murray, Gent.

Appraisement of the Estate of Samuel Metcalfe in the County of Kings & Queens returned and Ordered to be Recorded.

List of Tithes taken by James Ross, Gent., returned.

Ordered that the Sheriff summon 24 of the most capable freeholders of this County, not being Ordinary keepers, Constables, Surveyors of Highways, or owners or occupations of a Mill to appear at next November Court to serve as Grand Jury of Inquest for the Body of this County.

List of Tithes taken by Henry Vass, Gent., returned.

Charles Howerton, Guardian of Susanna Mountague, rendered an amount of the profits of her Estate to wch. he made Oath and the same was examined and approved of by the Court and Ordered to be Recorded.

William Thurston, Guardian of John Thurston, rendered an Amount of the profits of his Estate to wch. he made Oath and the same was examined & approved of by the Court & Ordered to be Recorded.

James Mc Han, Guardian of Philip Ware, rendered an amount of the profits of his Estate to wch. he made Oath and the same was examined and approved of by the Court and Ordered to be Recorded.

William Brook, Guardian of William Mountague, rendered an amount of the profits of his Estate to wch. he made Oath and the same was examined and approved of by the Court and Ordered to be Recorded.

William Brook, Guardian of Jack Mountague, rendered an amount of the profits of his Estate to wch. he made Oath and the same was examined and approved of by the Court and Ordered to be Recorded.

Deed Poll from Andrew Davis to Elizabeth Davis was proved by the Oaths of the witnesses thereto and Ordered to be Recorded.

Philip Edwards Jones having produced an Account to the Court [can't read] he made Oath that he had attended five days as a witness for Joseph Gayle against Isaac Jones, therefore it is Ordered that the sd. Gayle pay the sd. Jones for travelling two hundred & twenty, according to Law and 12/6 for is [can't read].

James Lee, Guardian of Overton Daniel, rendered an amount of the profits of his Estate to wch. he made Oath and the same was examined and approved of by the Court and Ordered to be Recorded.

James Lee, Guardian of Bartholomew Daniel, rendered an amount of the profits of his Estate to wch. he made Oath and the same was examined and approved of by the Court and Ordered to be Recorded.

Page 13

Indenture from Thomas Crittenden & Caty, his wife, to William Bowden[?], Senr., with the Receipt thereon endorsed was ackn.d by the sd. Thomas & Caty to be their act & Deed and Ordered to be Recorded. The sd. Caty being first privately examined according to Law.

On the Motion of Warner Blake, it is Ordered that George Daniel, James Ross, and William Murray or any two of them settle the Admin. Amount of the Estate of William Robenson[?], dec'd, and divide the Estate among the several Claimants according to Law and make their report to next Court.

George Daniel and William Murray, Gent., are appointed Commissioners by this Court for to let the rebuilding the old Dragon Bridge in conjunction with the Commissioners appointed by the County Court of Gloucester and to advantage the letting the same to the lowest bidder, and that the undertaker keep the same in repair for seven years.

Henry Chowning is allowed till next Court to render his Guardian Amount.

James Mitchell is allowed till next Court to render his Guardian Amount.

Susanna Daniel is excused from rendering her Guardian Amount.

Daniel Dejarnat is allowed till next Court to render his Guardian Amount.

George Warwick is excused from rendering her Guardian Amount.

James Stiff is appointed Surveyor of the highways in this County in the room of John Hodges[?].

Presentment of the Grand Jury – The Commonwealth, Pltf., VS Ann Dudley & Sarah Hudgin, Deft., for reasons appearing to the Court these presents are dismissed.

Ordered that Sarah Chowning be summoned to appear at next Court to know what her [can't read] will take Admin. on the Estate of Thomas Chowning, dec'd.

Ralph Wormeley, Junr., Philip Ludwell Grymes, Robert Spratt and William Steptoe, Gent., are recommended to his Excellency Benjamin Harrison, Esqr., Gov., by the Court as proper persons to execute the Office of Justices of the Peace for this County.

On the Motion of George Bird, County Lieutenant of Middlesex against Charles Dudley, Collector of the Eleventh Class for raising money for the enlisting of Soldiers, ordered that the sd. motion be dismissed and that the sd. George do not pay and costs to the Deft.

Thomas Healy, Guardian of Elizabeth Dillard, rendered an Account of the profits of her Estate to wch. he made Oath and the same was examined and approved of by the Court and Ordered to be Recorded.

Page 14

Thomas Healy made Oath to the Justices for the Specific Tax for the year 1782.

Ordered that the Court be adjourned to the Court in Course. The minutes of these proceedings were signed by Geoe. Daniel, Gent.

At a Court held for Middlesex County at the Courthouse in Urbanna on Monday the 27th day of October 1783

Present – George Daniel, Thomas Segar, John George, James Ross, Gent.

On the Petition of Agrippa Dunn, it is Ordered that Thomas Turner be summoned to appear at next Court to show cause if any he hath why the sd. Dunn shall not have a Cartway through the sd. Tuner's land to the main Road.

Deed Poll from John Jackson, Senr. with the receipt thereon endorsed to Adam Aldridge, was proved to be the Act and Deed of the sd. John by the Oath of the witnesses thereto and Ordered to be Recorded.

Henry Chowning is excused from sending his Guardian Amount of the Orphans of William Taylor until next August.

Absent – John George, Gent. Present – Henry Vass, Gent.

Deed from Thomas Patterson & Elizabeth, his wife, with the Receipt thereon endorsed to John George, Gent., was ackn.d and Ordered to be Recorded, she sd. Elizabeth being first privately examined according to Law.

Overton Cosby is appointed Ballast Master of the Port of Rappahannock at Urbanna.

William Jones, Guardian of Lucy Clare, rendered an Account of the profits of her Estate to wch. he made Oath and the same was examined and approved of by the Court and Ordered to be Recorded.

Letters of Administration with the Will annexed is granted to Sarah Chowning on the Estate of Thomas Chowning, dec'd, the sd. Sarah having taken the Oath of Admin. and entered into and ackn.d her Bond with Henry Chowning and Nelson Daniel her Securities in the penalty of £1,000 with Condition according to Law.

Ordered William Chowning, Tobias Allen, Harry Beverley Yates, and John Daniel, or any three being first sworn bef. some Justice of the Peace for the County do appraise the Estate of Thomas Chowning, dec'd and make their report to the next Court.

16

Lucy & Fanny Jones, Orphans of Isaac Jones, came to Court and chose William Hackney, their Guardian, he with William Churchill, his security, and [can't read] and ackn.d their Bond with the penalty of £2,000 with Condition according to Law.

Page 15

The Court has appointed William Hackney, Guardian of Elizabeth Jones, Orphan of Isaac Jones, he with William Churchill, his security, and he entered and ackn.d their Bond with the penalty of £1,000 with Condition according to Law.

Gabriel Jones, Orphan of Isaac Jones, came into Court and chose William Jones, his Guardian, the sd. William and James Dunlevy & Charles Edwards, his securities entered and ackn.d their Bond with the penalty of £2,000 with Condition according to Law.

The Court appointed William Jones, Guardian of Isaac Jones, Orphan of Isaac Jones, he with James Dunlevy & Charles Edwards, his securities entered and ackn.d their Bond with the penalty of £2,000 with Condition according to Law.

In Debt – Robert Ware, Senr., Pltf., VS John Thurston, Deft., for £7, 10 shillings due by Bond under the hand and seal of the sd. Deft. as is set forth in the Declaration the sd. Deft. this day appeared and confessed Judgment. Therefore, it is considered by the Court that the sd. Pltf. recover against the Deft. £7, 10 shillings and costs. But this Judgment to be discharged by the payment of £3, 18 shillings with legal interest thereon to be computed from 18 Apr 1783 till paid and the costs and lawyer's fee. Memo – the Pltf. agrees to stay execution and the Judgment till the [?] day of March next.

On the Motion of John George, Gent., for leave to erect a water grist mill on his land and swamp called Mickelburrough's, the sd. George holding the lands on both sides of the sd. swamp. It is therefore Ordered by the Court that the Sheriff Summon a Jury to view and ascertain the damages that may occur to any person or power by erecting the sd. Mill and make their report to this Court.

Ordered that Jon Craine Gosler, of Middlesex County, hire out Davy, a Negro Slave, who says he belongs to Colonel Thomas Sumpter, of South Carolina, and the sd. hire to apply to discharging the Prison fee for the sd. Slave according to Law.

Absent – Thomas Segar, Gent. Present – John George, Gent.

Ordered that this Court be adjourned to the Court in Course. The minutes of these proceedings were signed by George Daniel, Gent.

At a Court held for Middlesex County at the Courthouse in Urbanna on Monday the 24th day of November 1783

Present – George Daniel, Thomas Segar, John George, James Ross, and Thomas Roane, Gent.

Ordered the list of Tithes belonging to Ralph Wormeley and Joseph Hardee beaded to the General list.

Page 16

Harry Beverley Yates, James Dunlevy, Daniel Dejarnatt, Anderson [can't read], John Owen, Churchill Blakey, John Morgan, John Adkerson, Aquippa Dunn, Ambrose Kenneday, Thomas Brooks, William Jones, Junr., Daniel Stringer, Richard Bristow, Nicholas Tuggle, & Simon Laughlin were sworn a Grand Jury of Inquest for the Body of this County, and having received their Charge, retired from the Barr to consult of their verdict, and after sometime returned unto Court, and made the following punishments, to wit.: John Clark for **one Negro wench** in his list of Tithes; John Wake for concealing all his Taxable property, viz. – two Negroes, 18 head of cattle, and his list of Tithes; Robert Wake for his list of Tithes; the Overseer of the road from Coll. Churchill's Mill to the Trap; Kenny Mickelburrough's Estate for its list of Tithes; Griffin Tuggle for his Taxable property and the Estate of William Brooks; Hugh Walker for his list of Tithes; Edmund Berkeley for his list of Tithes and Taxable property; the Estate of George Lorimer for his list of Tithes; John Groom[?] for Tithes; Sarah Parker for a bastard Child; Nancy [can't read] for a bastard Child; William Elliot for his list of Tithes; Matthew Elliot for his list of Tithes; William Churchill for his Tithes & the number of his cattle; James Jeffre[?] for one Tithe; John Meders[?] for his Taxable property; John Seward for his Taxable property; the Surveyor of the Road from Dillard's Ordinary to the Essex Line; the Surveyor of the road from Mickelburrough's bridge to James Kidd's; the Surveyor of the road from Corbin's Mill to Neilson Mill; Henry Lynn for his list of Tithes and Taxable property; James Peter for his Tithe; George Blake, Senr. for one Tithe; Joanna Wake for 3 tithes; John Sole for one Tithe; John Cornelius for his Tithe & Taxable property; George West for one Tithe; John Jackson in pine lot for his Tithables; John Crosby for two Tithes; Mary Bird for her Overseer; Charles Fleming for his Tithes; the Estate of Beverley Daniel for the list of Tithes; Lucy Jones for 2 Tithes; and the Grand Jury having nothing further to present was discharged.

Ordered that the several persons presented by the Grand Jury be summoned to appear at the next Court.

18

Present – Philip Mountague, Gent. Absent - John George, Gent.

Letters of Administration granted to Samuel Klug, Clerk, on the Estate of George Lorimer, dec'd, he having taken the Oath of an Administration and entered into Bond with Philip Ludwell Grymes & George Daniel, is Securities in the penalty of £20,000.

Ordered that George Daniel, Philip Ludwell Grymes, James Ross and Ralph Wormeley, Junr., or any three of them being first sworn bef. some Justice of the Peace for the County, do appraise the Estate of George Lorimer, dec'd, and make their report to the next Court.

James Dunlevy, Guardian of James Faulkner, Orphan of John Faulkner, rendered this Account of the profits of her Estate to wch. he made Oath and the same was examined and approved of by the Court and Ordered to be Recorded.

Ordered that the list of Tithes belonging to John Jackson, Junr., Daniel Dejarnatt & Thomas Taff be added to the general list.

Absent – Philip Mountague, John George, Gent. Present – George Daniel, Gent.

The last Will and testament of Elizabeth Reade, dec'd was presented in Court [continued next page]

Page 17

and proved by the Oaths of William Bristow, Junr. and Harry Beverley Yates, two of the witnesses thereto and ordered to be Recorded.

Ordered that Thomas Taff's list of taxable property be added to the general list.

Letters of Administration is granted to Francis Corbin on the Estate of James Corbin, dec'd, he having taken the Oath of an Administrator and entered into Bond with William Churchill and George Daniel his securities in the penalty of £45,000 with Condition according to Law.

Ordered that George Bird, Philip Mountague, Thomas Segar and Harry Beverley Yates or any two of them being first sworn bef. some Justice of the Peace for the County do appraise the Estate of Gavin Corbin, dec'd, and make their report to the next Court.

Indenture from Francis Oliver and Ann, his wife, with the receipt thereon endorsed to John Groome, was ackns. to be their Act and Deed and Ordered to be recorded, the sd. Ann being first privately examined according to Law.

Absent – James Ross, Gent. Present – Henry Vass, Gent.

Ordered that Overton Cosby, Elliot Sturman, Jonathan Dennison & James Ross, or any three of them, do meet and settle the Administration Amount of the Estate of Bartholomew Yates, Junr., and make their report to this Court.

Ordered that Overton Cosby, Elliot Sturman, Jonathan Dennison & James Ross, or any three of them, settle the Administration Amount of the Estate of Jane Blackley, and make their report to this Court.

Indenture from Samuel Greenwood and Sibel, his wife, with the receipt thereon endorsed to Francis Oliver, was proved to be their Act and Deed, by the oaths of Philip Mountague, John George, and John Mullins, three of the witnesses, wch. together with a Commission of the sd. Sebil giving examination was returned and ordered to be Recorded.

Letters of Administration on the Estate of William Daniel, dec'd, is granted to Hannah Daniel, she having taken the Oath of the Administrix, and entered into Bond with William Wood, her security in the penalty of £500 with Condition according to Law.

Ordered that William Robinson, William Dean, James Dunlevy and Charles Robinson, or any three of them, being first sworn bef. a Justice of the Peace for this County, do appraise the Estate of William Daniel, dec'd, and make their report to the next Court.

Letters of Administration on the Estate of Benjamin Medaris, dec'd, is granted to James Lee, he having taken the Oath of an Administrator, entered into Bond in the penalty of five hundred [?] with Condition according to Law.

Ordered that Philp Mountague, Thomas Mountague, William Mountague & John Rilee[?], or any three of them, being first sworn bef. a Justice of the Peace for this County, do appraise the Estate of Benjamin Mederas, dec'd, and make their report to the next Court.

Page 18

Ordered that John Hodges and William Stiff be added to the former Order of this Court for settling the Administration Amount of the Estate of Joseph Pritchard, dec'd.

Letters of Administration is granted to Thomas Realy on the Estate of Thomas Willis, he having taken the Oath of an Administrator, with Conditions according to Law.

Ordered that Lawrence Meacham, John Mickelburrough, John Brooks and James Piggot, or any three of them, being first sworn bef. a Justice of Peace for this County, do appraise the Estate of Thomas Willis, dec'd, and make their report to the next Court.

Present – Overton Cosby & James Ross, Gent.

Ordered that George Bird, Gent., do let the repairing of the Prison in this County to lowest bidder and that the same be done in a workman-like manner.

Order that John Thunowgood be summoned to appear at the next Court to be held for the County to know whether he will undertake the Executorship of the Estate of the late Elizabeth Reade, dec'd.

Jacob Owen is appointed to Surveyor of the Highways in this County in the room of Samuel Wood.

Lawrence Meacham common bail for Griffin Tuggle at the Suit of James Lee brought the sd. Tuggle into Court and delivered him up into custody.

Ordered that this Court be adjourned to the Court in Course.

The minutes of these proceedings were signed by Philip Mountague, Gent.

At a Court held for Middlesex County at the Courthouse in Urbanna on Monday the 22th day of December 1783

Present – George Daniel, Thomas Segar, John George, Overton Cosby, James Ross, and William Murray.

Edmund Berkeley, Gent., took the Oath of Justice of the Peace and also the Oath of a Justice of Peace of Oyer and Terminer.

Ordered that Thomas Segar, William Owen, Junr., Henry Vass, Senr., and John Jackson, Junr., do view the road from Ware's bridge to the Crooked Tree that William Bowden wants to turn betw. him the sd. Bowden & Thomas Segar and report to the next Court the conveniences and inconveniences to will arise[?] to the publick.

Present – Edmund Berkeley, Gent.

Ordered that John Morgan, James Dunlevy, Dudley Vaughan, & John Hodges, or any three of them, do meet and settle the administration Account of the Estate of Isaac Jones, dec'd, and divide his Estate among the several Claimants, according to hi Will and make their report to the next Court.

Ordered that James Ross, Elliot Sturman, & Jonathan Dennison be added to the former order of this Court for dividing the Estate of Beverley Daniel, dec'd.

Absent - George Daniel and John George, Gent.

Page 19

Commonwealth agst. Griffin Tuggle, [can't read]

Commonwealth agst. [?] L. Walker, dismissed but his Tithes to be added.

Commonwealth agst. George Lorimer, Admin., dismissed but his Tithes to be added.

Present – Henry Vass & John George, Gent. Absent – Edmund Berkly, Gent.

Commonwealth agst. Edmund Berkeley, Gent., dismissed but Tithes to be added.

Commonwealth agst. William Elliot dismissed but his Tithes to be added.

Commonwealth agst. William Churchill dismissed but his Tithes to be added.

Commonwealth agst. Jane Jessee dismissed but his Tithes to be added.

Commonwealth agst. John Clark dismissed but his Tithes to be added

Absent – Henry Vass and Overton Cosby, Gent.

Commonwealth agst. Francis Oliver dismissed.

Commonwealth agst. George Blake, Senr., dismissed but his Tithes to be added.

Commonwealth agst. Joanna Wake dismissed but her Tithes to be added.

Commonwealth agst. John Sole dismissed.

Commonwealth agst. John Cornelius dismissed but his Tithes to be added.

Commonwealth agst. George West dismissed.

Commonwealth agst. John Jackson dismissed but his Tithes to be added.

Commonwealth agst. Mary Bird dismissed but his Tithes to be added.

Commonwealth agst. Charles Fleming dismissed but his Tithes to be added.

Commonwealth agst. Molley Daniel dismissed but his Tithes to be added.

Commonwealth agst. Lucy Jones dismissed.

Commonwealth agst. Matthew Elliot dismissed but his Tithes to be added.

Thomas Patterson is appointed Surveyor of the highways in the room of Francis Oliver.

John Healy is appointed Surveyor of the highways in room of Robert Mc Tyre.

Isaac Carlton produced a Commission to the Court from his Excellency Benjamin Harrison, Esqr., Gov. of VA, appointing his Surveyor of this County, the sd. Carlton took the Oath of a Surveyor and he with [can't read rest of the bottom of the page].

Page 20

Ordered Thomas Segar, [can't read] Dejarnatt, or nay of the three of them to know the lands of Thomas [can't read] and make their report to this Court of the conveniences and inconveniences that may that may occur to the sd. Turner by Agrippa Dunn having a cartway through the sd. Turner's land.

Appraisement of the Estate of Thomas Willis, dec'd returned and Ordered to be Recorded.

Present – Overton Cosby, Gent.

Motion for not paying the Soldier Money - George Bird, County Lieut. agst John Roane & Simon Laughlin, for reasons appearing to the Court, the sd. Motion is dismissed.

Ordered that the Church Wardens bind out Nilson Parry according to Law.

Ordered that the Court be adjourned to the Court in Course.

The minutes of these proceedings were signed by Edmund Berkeley, Gent.

At a Court held for Middlesex County at the Courthouse in Urbanna on Monday the 26th day of January 1784

Present – Edmund Berkeley, Henry Vass, John George, Overton Cosby and James Ross, Gent.

James Gregorie this day produced a Certificate of his being a Citizen of the State of South Carolina under the hand of the Gov. and the seal of the sd. State and the same was ordered to be Recorded.

Tobias Allen and Robert Murray produced a Commission from his Excellency Benjamin Harrison, Gov. of the State, appointing them Inspectors of Tobacco at the public Warehouse in Urbanna. The sd. Allen and Murray having taken the Oath prescribed by Law, entered into Bond with Harry Beverley Yates and William Churchill, their securities in the penalty of £1,000 according to Law.

On the motion of Henry Vass, Gent., it is ordained that the Clerk certify to his Excellency the Gov., that George Bird, Gent., who is first mentioned in the former recommendation of this Court, has served two years as Sheriff for the County and that the sd Henry Vass is the next mentioned in the sd. Recommendation

Letters of Administration are granted to Tobias Allen on the Estate of Reuben Allen, dec'd, the sd. Allen having taken the Oath of an Administration and entered into Bond with Thomas Healy, his security, in the penalty of £500 according to Law.

By Attachment – Robert Spratt, Pltf. VA Griffin Tuggle, Pltf., came the Pltf. by his Attorney and the sd. Deft. not appearing although solemnly called came not whereupon the Pltf. having [can't read] Oath to the [can't read-continued next page]

Page 21

[continued from previous page] Account. It is considered by the Court that the sd. Pltf. [can't read] against the sd. Deft. £3, 17 shillings and his costs..

By Attachment – Robert Spratt, Pltf. VA Griffin Tuggle, Pltf., came the Pltf. by his Attorney and the sd. Deft. not appearing although solemnly called came, therefore it is considered by the Court that the sd. Platf recover against the sd. Deft. £45, 8 shillings. 4 pence half penny with legal interest to be computed from the 26th April 1774 till paid and the costs.

24

Ordered William Chowning, Henry Beverley Yates, Robert Stamper and James Kidd or any three of them being first sworn bef. some Justice of the peace for this County, do appraise the Estate of Reuben Allen, dec'd, and make their report to the next Court.

Letters of Administration is granted to James Gregorie on the Estate of John Adair, dec'd, he having taken the Oath of an Administrator and entered into Bond with Overton Cosby his security in the penalty of £100 according to Law.

Frances and Ann Mikelburrough, Orphans of Edmund Mickelburrough, came to Court and chosen John Mickelburrough their Guardian, the sd. John with John Daniel, his security entered into and ackn.d their Bond in the penalty of £500 with Condition according to Law.

Robert Stamper produced a Commission from his Excellency Benjamin Harrison, Gove. of this state, appointing him an additional Inspector of Tobacco at the public Warehouse in Urbanna, the sd. Stamper with Thomas Healy, his security entered into and ackn.d their Bond in the penalty of £500 with Condition according to Law.

Tobacco as a Commutable is valued by the Court according to Law at 30 shillings per hundred.

Ordered that is Court be adjourned to the Court in Course.

The Minutes of the proceedings were signed by Edmund Berkeley, Gent.

At a Court held for Middlesex County at the Courthouse in Urbanna on Monday the 22nd day of March 1784

Present – Edmund Berkeley, George Daniel, Thomas Segar, James Vass, Gent.

Thomas Segar, Gent., is appointed for the upper precinct in this County to be take a list of all white males and mulatto free persons above the age of 21 years, and all Slaves, horses, mares, colts, stud horses, cattle, wheel carriages and Billiard Tables and make return agreeable to the Act of Assembly, Thomas Roane, Gent., is appointed for the Middle Precinct and [can't read].

Page 22

Ordered that the Sheriff summon 24 freeholders not being Constables, Overseers of the highways, owners of[or?] occupiers of water Mills to serve as a body of Inquest for this County to appear next May Court.

Indenture from Robert Thurston and Peggy, his wife, with the receipt thereon endorsed with memorandum of livery & [seizen[?] to Thomas Crittenden was proved by the oaths of Benjamin Sewards and John Sewards, two of the witnesses thereto to be their Act and Deed of the sd. Robert , wch. together with the Commission for the privy examination of the sd. Peggy returned and Ordered to be Recorded.

Indenture from Robert Thurston and Peggy, his wife, with the receipt thereon endorsed with memorandum of livery & [seizen[?] to George Saunders was proved by the oaths of Harry Beverley Yates and Thomas Chowning, two of the witnesses thereto to be their Act and Deed, wch. together with the Commission for the privy examination of the sd. Peggy returned and Ordered to be Recorded.

A Claim of Charles Lee for 225 pounds of beef, also for one cart and two men for one day for the Army in Gloster impressed by Paul Thelman are allowed as form. by the Court.

Absent – George Daniel. Present – John George, Gent.

Daphne belonging to Jane Dudley is set County levy free by the Court.

The last Will and Testament of Rachel Murray, dec'd, was presented in Court by George Daniel and Thomas Roane, two of the, therein named, who made Path according to Law and the same was proved by the Oaths of the Witnesses thereto and Ordered to be Recorded and on the motion of the sd. certificate was granted them for obtaining a Probate in due form, giving security, whereupon they with Thomas Segar and William Murray, their securities entered into and ackn.d their Bond in the penalty of £1,000 with condition according to law.

Middlesex County – Debt. Lf. Tobacco

To William Churchill, Clerk, for one year service		1248
To Do. for his amount in cash	£5.9.0	
To George Bird, Gent., Sheriff for one year service		1248
To Thomas Moore, Deputy Attorney 1 yr. salary		1040
To John Craine for keeping ferry over Urbanna Creek for one year		2500
To Do. for keeping the Court House and making fires		750
To William Churchill for Copies of the List of Souls		200
To William Bristow for his amount against the County	£0.10.9	
To James Lee for his amount		287.5
To cash for the Dragon Bridge	£16.0.0	
To 2,500 lb of Tobacco for to pay cash debts		2500
By a deposit item in the Sheriff Hands – 19 lb Tobacco		

26

To the Sheriff for collecting 9754.5 Tobacco
By 1267 Tithes @ 8.5 [?] Tobacco tithes 10,452.75

Page 23

By a Deposition in the Sheriff's hands to be answered for at the laying the next
Levy 113.5 lb. Tobacco. The Levy for this present year is 8.5 Tobacco lb. poll
Ordered that the Sheriff collect the same from each Tithable person in this and
pay the same to the several Creditors.

Ordered that Edmund Berkeley & George Daniel, Gent., do examine the Clerk
Office and make their Return to this Court.

Ordered that Thomas Segar, Gent, do make up and render his Account against
this County for the purchasing a wagon harness and Tilt to next Court.

**In Chancery - Thomas Roane and Sally his wife, Harry Beverley Yates and
Lucy his wife & Catharine Murray, Complt. VS Deft. It is Ordered and
decreed that Edmund Berkeley, Overton Cosby, Philip Ludwell Grymes,
William Churchill, James Ross, and Robert Spratt, or any three of them, do
divide two-thirds of the Negroes wch. descended to William Murray, heir at
Law to John Murray, dec'd, and allot so many of them to the several
Complainants as shall be sufficient to discharge their respective
proportionable parts of the appraised value of the sd. Negroes according to
the Prayer of the Bill and make their report to the next Court.**

Ordered that the former order of this Court for repairing the Prison be set aside
and that George Bird and Thomas Segar. Gent., do let the repairing of the prison
to some workman and that he bring in his Account to this Court at the laying the
next Levy.

Ordered that John George, James Kidd, Robert Stamper, and Maurice Smith or
any three of them do divide the legacy to the Children of Edmund
Mickelburrough by the Will of Henry Mickelburrough, dec'd, and make their
report to next Court.

Indenture from Matthew Mc Han and Mary his wife, with the receipt thereon
endowed to William Shepard, was proved to be their Act and Deed by the oaths
of Henry Vass, Philip Mountague, and Henry Vass, Junr. & three witnesses
thereto & ordered to be recorded.

The last Will and testament of Christopher Robinson was presented in Court and
proved by the Oath of Samuel Klug, Clerk, one of the witnesses thereto and who
made Oath that he saw Elizabeth Reade and Nathaniel Carpenter, and James

Mickelburrough, the other witnesses thereto, subscribe the same in the presence of the Testator and the sd. Will is Ordered to be Recorded.

Letters of Administration with the Will of Elizabeth Reade, dec'd, is granted to Charles Reade, the sd. Charles having taken the Oath of an Administrator and entered into Bond with Charles Curtis and James Kidd, his securities, in the penalty of £1,000 according to Law.

Ordered that James Kidd, John George, Maurice Smith and Robert Stamper, or any three of them, being first sworn bef. a Justice of peace of this County do appraise the Estate of Elizabeth Reade and make report to next Court.

Page 24

Letters of Administration is granted to Samuel Klug, Clerk, on the un-administered estate of Mary Elizabeth Thacker, he having taken the Oath of an Administrator and entered into Bond with William Churchill, his Security, in the penalty of £10,000 with Condition according to law.

Indenture from Thomas Tombs and Mary, his wife, to Charles Edwards was proved by the Oath of Maurice Smith and William Curtis to be the Act & Deed of the sd. Thomas, wch. together with a Commission for the privy examination of the sd. Mary returned and Ordered to be Recorded.

Division of the Estate of Beverley Daniel returned and ordered to be Recorded.

Ordered that the Clerk certify that George Saunders has been twice taxed.

Ordered that Maurice Smith, Robert Murray, Benjamin Bristow, and James Kidd, or any three of them, being first sworn bef. a Justice of peace of this County do appraise the Estate of Rachel Murray and make report to next Court.

Henry Vass, Gent.., having produced a Commission from his Excellency Benjamin Harrison, Gov, appointing him Sheriff, of this County, took the Oath of Sheriff, the sd. Henry Vass with Philip Mountague and Thomas Segar, his securities, entered into and ackns. their Bond in the penalty of £1,000 with Condition according to Law.

Deed of Gift from Charles Grymes to Jane Grymes, daughter of Philip Ludwell Grymes, was proved by the Oath of the witness thereto & ordered to be Recorded.

Division of the Estate of George Davis returned and Ordered to be recorded.

Division of the Estate of James Mountague returned and Ordered to be recorded.

Ordered that George Bird, Henry Vass, Philip Mountague and Churchill Blakey, or any three of them, do allot to Sarah Cloudas, late widow of Robert Daniel, her third part of the sd. Robert's Estate and make their report to next Court.

Ordered that Ralph Wormeley and Richard Corbin, Esqrs., of Christopher Robinson, dec'd, be summoned to appear at next Court to say whether they will qualify as to the Will.

Indenture from George Dillard with the receipt thereon endorsed to James Lee was proved to be the Act and Deed of the sd. George by the Oaths of the witnesses thereto and Ordered to be Recorded.

Indenture from Robert Mc Tyre with the receipt thereon endorsed to James Lee was proved by the Oaths of George Dillard and Reuben Lee to be the Act and Deed of the sd. Robert and ordered to be Recorded.

John George, Gent., is appointed a Commissioner for the valuing of the lands in this County in the room of Robert Daniel, Gent., dec'd.

Page 25

Indenture of Robert Corbin, Esqr., to Francis Corbin was proved by the Oaths of the witnesses thereto and Ordered to be Recorded.

Thomas Healy and John Healy were this day sworn under Sheriff for this County.

Absent – Thomas Roane. Present – Overton Cosby, Gent.

Jack Murray, Orphan of John Murray, dec'd, came into Court and chose Thomas Roane, Gent, his Guardian, the sd. Roane with William Munay[Murray?], his Security, entered into and ackn.d their Bond in the penalty of £1,000 with Condition according to Law.

Ordered that this Court be adjourned until to Morrow 10 o'clock.

The minutes of these proceedings were signed by Edmund Berkeley, Gent.

At a Court held for Middlesex County at the Courthouse in Urbanna on Tuesday the 23rd day of March 1784

Present – Edmund Berkeley, George Daniel, Overton Cosby, James Ross, Gent.

Pursuant to Law, it is Ordered the Overton Cosby, Gent., view the scales and examine and try the weights at the public Ware – house at Urbanna and if the sd. scales and weights be found deficient or differing from the Lawful Standard, that they cause the same to be repaired and mended and the weights to be made conformable to the Standard.

Order that the Standard Weights and Measures belonging to this County be delivered to Overton Cosby, Gent.

In Case – Samuel Chowning, Pltf. VS Charlotte Neilson, Deft., came as well the Pltf. by his attorney as the Deft. by her attorney and the sd. Deft. prays and has leave to Imparle here till the next Court then to led.

By Petition - Richard Bray, Pltf., VS Edward Brooks, Deft., is continued till next Court.

By Petition - Richard Bray, Pltf. VS Thomas Crittenden and Richard Cardwell, Deft., is continued till next Court.

In Debt - Richard Bray, Pltf. VS Edward Didlake & John Gardner, Deft.

Pages 26

The Deft. Edward Didlake being arrested and not appearing tho Solemnly called on the motion of the Pltf. by Benjamin Dabney, his attorney, it is Ordered that Judgment be entered against the Deft. and John Healy, his common bail for the Debt in the declaration mentioned unless the sd. Deft. shall appear at the next Court, give Special bail & plead to Issue and as to the other Deft. Gardner, the Suit abates by return.

In Debt - Richard Bray, Pltf., VS Robert Thurston & Mary Ware, Deft., the Deft Mary Ware being arrested and not appearing tho Solemnly called on the motion of the Pltf. by Benjamin Dabney, his attorney, it is Ordered that Judgment be entered against the Deft. and George Bird, Sheriff of the County, for the debt in the declaration mentioned unless the sd. Deft. shall appear at the next Court, give Special bail & plead to Issue. The Suit abates as to Thurston, the other Deft. by his death.

In Case - Robert Singleton, Pltf., VS Thomas Saunders, Deft., the Suit is dismissed by Pltf. Order.

In Case - Isaac Singleton, Pltf. VS Dudley Vaughan, Deft., the Deft not being arrested and not appearing tho Solemnly called on the motion of the Pltf. an Attachment is granted him returnable to the next Court.

In Case - Edward Conner, Pltf., VS George Lorimer, Deft., the Suit abates by the Deft. death.

In Case - Harry Beverley Yates, Pltf., VS John Montague, Exec. of James Montague, Deft., This Suit abates by return.

In Case - Robert Matthew, Pltf., VS Zachariah Shackelford, Deft., the Deft. not appearing tho Solemnly called on the motion of the sd. Pltf. by Benjamin Dabney, his attorney, it is Ordered that Judgment be entered against the Deft. and George Bird, Sheriff, for the Debt in the declaration mentioned unless the sd. Deft. shall appear at the next and given Special bail & plead to Issue.

In Debt - William & Bartholomen Bristow, Pltf., VS Samuel Chowning and James Boyd, Deft.

Page 27

The Deft. being arrested and not appearing tho Solemnly called on the motion of the Pltf. by Thomas Moore, their attorney, it is Ordered that Judgment be entered against the Deft. and Charles Collier & Daniel Dejarnatt, their common bail for Debt in the declaration mentioned unless the said Deft. shall appear at the next Court, give Special bail & plead to Issue.

In Debt - William and Bartholomew Bristow, Plft. VS Robert Thurston, Deft., this Suit abates by Deft. death.

In Debt - William and Bartholomew Bristow, Plft. VS Robert Curtis & Charles Curtis, Deft., being arrested and not appearing tho Solemnly called on the motion of the Pltf. by Thomas Moore, their attorney, it is Ordered that Judgment be entered against the Deft. William Curtis, their common bail for Debt in the declaration mentioned unless the said Deft. shall appear at the next Court, give Special bail & plead to Issue.

In Debt - William & Bartholomew Bristow, Pltf. VS Thomas Gains & James Wortham, Deft., abates by return.

In Debt - William and Bartholomew Bristow, Plft. VS William Bristow and Robert Thurston, Deft., being arrested and not appearing tho Solemnly called on the motion of the Pltf. by Thomas Moore, their attorney, it is Ordered that Judgment be entered against the Deft., and George Bird, Sheriff of this County for the debt in the declaration mentioned unless the sd. Deft. shall appear at the next Court and give special bail and plead to Issue, this Suit abates as Thurston the other Deft. by his death.

In Debt - William and Bartholomew Bristow, Plft. VS Thomas Crittenden and Robert Thurston, Deft., Thomas Crittenden being arrested and not appearing tho Solemnly called on the motion of the Pltf. by Thomas Moore, their attorney, it is Ordered that Judgment be entered against the Deft., Thomas and Oliver Yarrington, his common bail, for the debt in the declaration mentioned unless the sd. Deft. shall appear at the next Court and give special bail and plead to Issue, this Suit abates as to Thurston by his death.

By Petition - William Bartholomew Bristow, Pltf. VS William Robinson and Warner Blake, Deft., continued till next Court.

Page 28

In Debt - Cary Kemp, assignee of William Murray, Pltf. VS William Moore, continued till next Court.

For Assault - Dennis Burn, Pltf. VS George Furnell, Deft. , the Deft. not being arrested on the motion of the Pltf. by Thomas Moore his attorney as Alias Capia is awarded the sd. Pltf. agst. the sd. Deft. returnable here at the next Court.

In Debt – Robert Mc Tyre, Pltf. VS. Joseph Hardee & Robert Thurston, Deft., The Deft. Hardee not being arrested and not appearing tho Solemnly called on the motion of the Pltf. by his attorney an attachment is awarded the sd. Pltf. against the sd. Deft. returnable here at the next Court, this suit abates as to Thurston by his death.

By Petition - Thomas Williams, Pltf. VS John Montague, of James Montague, Deft., this abates by Pltf. death.

On Scire Facias – James Lee, Pltf., VS Samuel Chowning, Deft., on the Scire Facias brought by James Lee against the Deft., this day came the parties by their attorneys, and the Deft. relinquishing his former plea says he cannot deny the Pltf. action nor but that he detains from him the money and tobacco in his Write of Scire Facias mentioned, therefore it is considered that the Pltf. have execution against the Deft. for £24, 10 shillings, with interest thereon from the 1st April 1774 till paid and 112 lbs. of Tobacco and 16 shillings, 3 pence and also the costs for suing forth and prosecuting this Writ.

In Case – James Semple, Admin. of James Hart, Pltf. VS John Robinson, of Peter Robinson, dec'd, Deft., came as well the Pltf. by his attorney as the Deft. by his attorney and the sd. Deft. prays to have leave to Imparle here till the next Court and then to plead.

32

In Debt – James Gregorie & George Forman, of John Daniel, Pltf. VS Griffin Tuggle, Deft., The Deft. being arrested and not appearing tho Solemnly called on the motion of the sd. Pltf. by their attorney. It is Ordered that Judgment against the Deft. and his common bail for the Deft. in the declaration mentioned unless the Deft. shall appear at the next Court gives special bail [?] back and plead to Issue.

Page 29

In Case - John Clemons, Pltf. VS Simon Laughlin, Deft., the Deft. being arrested and not appearing tho Solemnly called on the motion of the sd. Pltf. by their attorney. It is Ordered that Judgment against the Deft. and his common bail for the Deft. in the declaration mentioned unless the Deft. shall appear at the next Court gives special bail [?] back and plead to Issue.

In Debt - James Lee, assignee of James Kidd, assignee of William Bristow, Pltf., VS John Kidd and Griffin Tuggle, Deft., dismissed by Pltf. Order.

By Petition - Benjamin Hackney, Pltf., VS John Kenningham, Deft., continued till next Court

In Debt - John Quarles assignee of Charles Stuart, Pltf. VS Rawleigh Jones, Deft., the Deft. being arrested and not appearing tho Solemnly called on the motion of the sd. Pltf. by his attorney. It is Ordered that Judgment be entered against the Deft. and George Bird, Sheriff of the County for the debt in the declaration mentioned unless the Deft. shall appear at the next, gives special bail and plead to Issue.

In Debt - John Jackson, Pltf. VS Robert Thurston & Alexander Bristow, Deft.. The Deft. Bristow being arrested and not appearing tho Solemnly called on the motion of the sd. Pltf. by his attorney. It is Ordered that Judgment be entered against the Deft. and George Bird, Sheriff of the County for the debt in the declaration mentioned unless the Deft. shall appear at the next, gives special bail and plead to Issue, abates as to Thurston by his Death.

In Case - Nelson Daniel, Pltf., VS George Lorimer, Deft., continued till next Court.

Carter Braxton, Pltf. VS John Montague, of James Montague, Deft., abates by return.

Page 30

In Case - William Mitchell, Pltf. VS Charles Grymes, Deft. The Deft. being arrested and not appearing tho Solemnly called on the motion of the sd. Pltf. by his attorney. It is Ordered that Judgment be entered against the Deft. and his common bail for this Debt in the Declaration mentioned unless the Deft. shall appear at the next Court, gives special bail and plead to Issue

In Debt - Jaquilen Ambler, as Sheriff of York County, Pltf. VS Charles Grymes & the of Lewis Burwell, dec'd, Deft. The Deft. being arrested and not appearing tho Solemnly called on the motion of the sd. Pltf. by his attorney. It is Ordered that Judgment be entered against the Deft. and his common bail for this Debt in the Declaration mentioned unless the Deft. shall appear at the next Court, gives special bail and plead to Issue. The suit abates as to Burwell, Execs. by return.

In Case - William Goosely, Pltf. VS Philip Ludwell Grymes, Deft. The Deft. being arrested and not appearing tho Solemnly called on the motion of the sd. Pltf. by his attorney. It is Ordered that Judgment be entered against the Deft. and George Bird, Sheriff of this County, for the Debt in the Declaration mentioned unless the Deft. shall appear at the next Court, gives special bail and plead to Issue.

In Debt - George Green & John Whiting, Pltf. VS Benjamin Deagle, Deft. The Deft. being arrested and not appearing tho Solemnly called on the motion of the sd. Pltf. by his attorney. It is Ordered that Judgment be entered against the Deft. and Andrew Davis, his common bail, for the Debt in the Declaration mentioned unless the Deft. shall appear at the next Court, gives special bail and plead to Issue

By Petition – George Green, Pltf. VS James Wortham, of Meacham Fearn[?], Deft., abates by Deft. Death.

In Debt – James Laughlin & Elizabeth, his wife, Pltf. VS William George and William Bristow, Deft., dismissed by Pltf. Order.

On Petition - William Clements, Pltf. VS Francis Woodley, Deft., continued for the Deft. till next Court.

By Assault - Elizabeth Blackburn, Pltf. VS Jonathan Herrin[?], Deft., continued.

Page 31

In Scire Facias - William Clayton, of John Clayton, Pltf. VS John Smith, of Augustine Smith, Deft., continued till next Court.

In Petition - James Lee, Admin., of Hannah Gill, Pltf. VS Thomas Richardson & William Jones, Deft., this day came the Pltf. by his attorney and the Deft. Jones by his attorney that he cannot deny the Pltf. action. Therefore, it is considered that the Pltf. recover against the sd. Jones £1, 13 shillings, 11 pence with Interest from 3 Oct 1771 till paid, and the Costs [can't read] 24 Jan 1772 received of William Jones 13 shillings & of Benjamin Bristow 2 shillings & 6 pence inpart of the within Bond.

On Petition by an old Judgment in Gloster Court - Benjamin Chen Crockett & Co., Pltf., VS George Jackson, Deft., the Deft. not appearing tho Solemnly called it is therefore considered by the Court that the Pltf. recover against the Deft. £3, 6 shillings, 3 pence, half penny. Also 63 lbs. of Tobacco and 7 shillings, 6 pence and their costs.

On Petition by an old Judgment in Gloster Court - Benjamin Chen Crockett & Co., Pltf., VS Reuben Layton, Deft., the Deft. not appearing tho Solemnly called it is therefore considered by the Court that the Pltf. recover against the Deft. £3, 6 shillings, 3 pence, half penny. Also 63 lbs. of Tobacco and 7 shillings, 6 pence and their costs.

Same VS John Boss, continued till next Court.

On Petition – George Blake, Pltf. VS William Moore, Deft., continued till next Court.

In Debt - Nelson Daniel, Pltf., VS Betty Kemp, Deft., the Deft. being arrested and not appearing tho Solemnly called on the motion of the sd. Pltf. by his attorney. It is Ordered that Judgment be entered against the Deft. and her Common bail for the Debt in the Declaration mentioned unless the Deft. shall appear at the next Court, gives special bail and plead to Issue.

In Case - Charles Lee, Junr., Pltf, VS John Montague, of James Montague, Deft., the Deft. being arrested and not appearing tho Solemnly called on the motion of the sd. Pltf. by his attorney. It is Ordered that Judgment be entered against the Deft. for the Debt in the Declaration mentioned unless the Deft. shall appear at the next Court, gives special bail and plead to Issue.

Page 32

In Case - Nelson Daniel, Pltf. VS Thomas Segar, Deft., the Deft. being arrested and not appearing tho Solemnly called on the motion of the sd. Pltf. by his attorney. It is Ordered that Judgment be entered against the Deft. and George Bird, Sheriff for the Debt in the Declaration mentioned unless the Deft. shall appear at the next Court, gives special bail and plead to Issue.

In Case - John New[?], of Daniel New, Pltf., VS Lucy Jones & Le Roy Peachey, of Lodowick Jones, Deft., abates by return.

In Case – Mary Robinson, Admin. of John Robinson, Pltf. VS Warner Blake, Deft., the Deft. being arrested and not appearing tho Solemnly called on the motion of the sd. Pltf. by his attorney. It is Ordered that Judgment be entered against the Deft. and George Bird, Sheriff for the Debt in the Declaration mentioned unless the Deft. shall appear at the next Court, gives special bail and plead to Issue.

In Case - Robert Price, of George Brooks, Pltf. VS William Thurston, Deft., the Deft. being arrested and not appearing tho Solemnly called on the motion of the sd. Pltf. by his attorney. It is Ordered that Judgment be entered against the Deft. and his common bail for the Debt in the Declaration mentioned unless the Deft. shall appear at the next Court, gives special bail and plead to Issue.

In Case - Charles Grymes, Pltf., VS Joseph Gayle, Deft., continued till next Court.

In Case – Daniel Stringer, Pltf. VS Henry Batchelder, Deft., continued till next Court.

In Case - William Jones, Pltf., VS George Bush, Deft., continued till next Court.

Page 33

[Can't be read] VS James Baker, Deft., the Deft. being arrested and not appearing tho Solemnly called on the motion of the sd. Pltf. by his attorney. It is Ordered that Judgment be entered against the Deft. and Sarah Baker, his common bail, for the Debt in the Declaration mentioned unless the Deft. shall appear at the next Court, gives special bail and plead to Issue.

In Debt - Christopher Tonkens, Pltf., VS Thomas Hanow[?] & John Jackson, Deft., being arrested and not appearing tho Solemnly called on the motion of the sd. Pltf. by his attorney. It is Ordered that Judgment be entered against the Deft. and his common bail for the Debt in the Declaration mentioned unless the Deft. shall appear at the next Court, gives special bail and plead to Issue.

In Case - William Elliot, Pltf., VS William Jones, Deft., Came as well as Pltf. by his attorney as the Deft. by his attorney and the sd. Deft. prays and has leave to Imparle here till the next Court and then to plead.

For Assault – Jonathan Herrin, Pltf. VS Paulin Blackburn, Deft., The Deft. not being arrested on the motion of the Pltf. by his attorney on alias Capias is awarded the sd. Pltf., against the sd. Deft., returnable here at the next Court.

In Case - Simon Laughlin, Pltf. VS Henry Lynn, Deft., this suit is dismissed by the Pltf. order.

In Case - Harry Beverley Yates, Pltf., VS John Montague, of James Mountague, dec'd, Deft., Came as well the Pltf. by his attorney and the Deft. by his attorney and the Deft. prays and has leave in Imparle here till the next Court and then to plead.

Agrippa Dunn agst. Thomas Turner, continued for report till next Court.

John George, Gent., his Petition for leave to build a water grist mill continued till next Court.

By Petition - Samuel Ernest, Pltf., VS Ralph Wormeley, Deft., this suit is continued till next Court.

In Case – William George assignee of Adam Charles Smith, Pltf. VS William Elliot, Deft. The Deft. being arrested and not appearing tho Solemnly called on the motion of the sd. Pltf. by his attorney. It is Ordered that Judgment be entered against the Deft. and Matthew Elliot, his common bail, for the Debt in the Declaration mentioned unless the Deft. shall appear at the next Court, gives special bail and plead to Issue.

Page 34

William Boxley, Pltf. VS Richard Corbin, Esqr., Deft., This Suit abates by return.

In Debt – Henry Purcell, of William Purcell, Pltf. VS Charles Fleming & George Green, Deft. The Deft Charles Fleming. being arrested and not appearing tho Solemnly called on the motion of the sd. Pltf. by his attorney. It is Ordered that Judgment be entered against the Deft. Charles and Matthew Elliot, his common bail, for the Debt in the Declaration mentioned unless the Deft. shall appear at the next Court, gives special bail and plead to Issue, this suit abates as to the other Deft. George Green by return..

[can't read] John Montague, of James Montague, dec'd, Pltf. VS Jonathan Dennison, Deft., came the Pltf as well by his attorney as the Deft. by his attorney and the sd. Deft. prays and has leave to Imparle here specially till the Court and then to plead.

In Case - William Segar, Pltf. VS Nelson Daniel, Deft., came as well the Pltf. by his attorney as the Deft. prays and has leave to Imparle here specially till the Court and then to plead.

In Debt - Benjamin Robinson, of Samuel Metcalf, dec'd, Pltf. VS Henry Batchelder and John Smith, Deft., the Deft Henry being arrested and not appearing tho Solemnly called on the motion of the sd. Pltf. by his attorney. It is Ordered that Judgment be entered against the Deft. Henry and George Bird, Gent., for the Debt in the Declaration mentioned unless the Deft. shall appear at the next Court, gives special bail and plead to Issue. An Alias Capias is awarded to the sd. Pltf. against the other Deft. Smith returnable here at the next Court.

In Debt - Benjamin Robinson, of Samuel Metcalf, dec'd, Pltf. VS Charles Grymes, Deft., this Suit is dismissed by the Pltf. Order.

John Muir, Pltf. VS [can't read the rest].

Page 35

[Continued from Page 34] The Deft being arrested and not appearing tho Solemnly called on the motion of the sd. Pltf. by his attorney. It is Ordered that Judgment be entered against the Deft. for the Debt in the Declaration mentioned unless the Deft. shall appear at the next Court, gives special bail and plead to Issue.

In Case - John Moultson, Pltf. VS Thomas Segar, Gent., Deft., the Deft. being arrested and not appearing tho Solemnly called on the motion of the sd. Pltf. by his attorney. It is Ordered that Judgment be entered against the Deft. and George Bird, Gent., Sheriff, for the Debt in the Declaration mentioned unless the Deft. shall appear at the next Court, gives special bail and plead to Issue.

In Debt - John Moultson, assignee of Robert Spratt assignee of Thomas Segar, Pltf. VS Harry Beverley Yates & Tobias Allen. Deft. being arrested and not appearing tho Solemnly called on the motion of the sd. Pltf. by his attorney. It is Ordered that Judgment be entered against the Deft. and George Bird, Gent., Sheriff, for the Debt in the Declaration mentioned unless the Deft. shall appear at the next Court, gives special bail and plead to Issue.

In Debt – John Davies, Pltf., VS Benjamin Hackney, Deft. Deft. being arrested and not appearing tho Solemnly called on the motion of the sd. Pltf. by his attorney. It is Ordered that Judgment be entered against the Deft. for the Debt in the Declaration mentioned unless the Deft. shall appear at the next Court, gives special bail and plead to Issue.

George Hanks, Pltf agst. Griffin Tuggle, Deft., by Order of the Court this suit is dismissed.

Frances Ross, Pltf., agst. John Hunt by Attachment by Order of Court this suit dismissed.

By Attachment - William Dance[?], Admin. of John Dance[?], Pltf. VS John Hunt, Deft. On the motion of the Pltf. by his attorney it is Ordered that Richard Dance as Gardishee[?] be summoned to appear at the next Court to render an amount of what assets he has in his hands belonging to the sd. John Hunt.

Charles Grymes, Pltf., agst. John Hunt, Deft., this Suit is dismissed by Order of the Court.

The Appraisement of the Estate of George Lorimer returned and Ordered to be Recorded.

Ordered that Peggy Thurston, widow of Robert Thurston, be summoned to appear at next Court to declare whether she will undertake the Admin. of the sd. Thurston Estate.

Ordered that Frances Wortham, widow of James Wortham, be summoned to appear at next Court to declare whether she will undertake the Admin. of the sd. Wortham Estate.

Ordered that the of Beverley Daniel deliver to the Clerk of this Court the book containing the surveys made by the sd. Beverley Daniel and those by Robert Daniel.

Ordered that this Court be adjourned to the Court in Course.

The minutes of this proceedings were signed by Edmund Berkeley, Gent.

Page 36

At a Court held for Middlesex County at the Courthouse in Urbanna on Monday the 26th day of April 1784

Present – Edmund Berkeley, George Daniel, Overton Cosby, James Ross, William Murray and Thomas Roane, Gent.

John George, Gent., took the Oath of Commissioner for the valuing of the lands in this County.

Edmund Berkeley, Gent., returned the list if Taxable Property taken by him.

A Claim of Henry Chowning for Beaves for 23 days, James Kidd for 23 days, Benjamin Kidd for 21 days, Edward Ware for 22 days, Churchill Blakey for 23 days, William Bristow for 19 days, Harry Beverley Yates for 6 days, Alexander Bristow for 13 days, Joseph Hardee for 6 days, John Cloudas for 3 days,

Thomas Crittenden for three days, the above persons are allowed by the Court 2 shillings per day for themselves and their horses.

Present John George, Gent.

This Court thinking themselves under the Constitution competent to the commendation of persons to act as Justices of the Peace in the sd. County, Do again recommend to His Excellency Benjamin Harrison, Gov., Ralph Wormeley, Junr., Philip Ludwell Grymes, Robert Spratt and William Staples, as proper persons to serve as Justices of the Peace for this County.

Present – Thomas Segar, Gent.

Indenture from James Lee to George Damon with receipt thereon endorsed was ackn.d by the sd. James to be his Act and Deed and Ordered to be Recorded.

Samuel Hugh Henry is recommended as a Man of probaty, honesty, and good demeanor by the Court to be the Gentleman appointed to examine the gentlemen applying for License to practice as Attorney's at Law agreeable to Act of Assembly.

Susanna Blake's Negro woman, Dinah, is set County Levy free.

Ordered that the Court be adjourned till tomorrow morning 10 o'clock. Te minutes of these proceedings were signed by Edmund Berkeley, Gent.

At a Court held for Middlesex County at the Courthouse in Urbanna on Monday the 27th day of April 1784

Present – Edmund Berkeley, George Daniel, Overton Cosby, John George, William Murray and James Ross, Gent.

Ordered that the Rev'd Samuel Klug, Clerk, Overton Cosby and James Ross, Gent., or any two of them, do examine the late Surveyor Books and deliver the same to the present Surveyor of this County and make their report to the Court

Ordered that the Sheriff of this County take the Estate of Henry Kidd into his hands and sell the land and make return according to Law to this Court.

Page 37

Ordered Tobias Allen, Henry Chowning, Henry Batchelder and Harry Beverley Yates, or any three of them, being first sworn bef. some Justice of the Peace for this County do appraise the Estate of Henry Kidd and make their report to next Court.

[An Order crossed out – can't be read.]

Ordered that the Sheriff of this County convene[?] a Jury to attend the Surveyor of the County to lay of the lines in dispute betw. Thomas Taff and Lewis Mountague, the sd. Taff having refused to have his lines [can't read] according to Law.

Petition for £2.10 sd. to be due by Account - Richard Bray, Pltf. VS Edward Brooks, Deft. This day came the Pltf. by his attorney and the Deft. not appearing, it is considered by the Court that the Pltf. against the Deft. £2, 10 shillings together with his Costs by him abt. this Suit expended[?].

On Petition - Richard Bray, Pltf. VS Thomas Crittenden & Richard Cardwell, Deft., for one pound, 18 shillings with legal interest from 1 Jan 1783 till paid under the hands and seals of the sd. Deft., as is set forth in the Petition, therefore it is considered by the Court that the sd. Pltf. recover against the sd. Deft., one pound, 18 shillings with legal interest together with his Costs by him abt. this Suit expended.

Present – Thomas Segar and James Ross, Gent. Absent – John George, Gent.

On Petition - William & Bartholomew Bristow, Pltf., VS William Robinson & Warner Blake, Deft., this Petition is dismissed by Pltf. order.

On Petition – William Clements, Pltf. VS Francis Woodley, Deft., this Petition is dismissed by Order of the Pltf.

Benjamin Chew Crockett & Co., Pltf., VS John Boss, Deft., for reasons appearing to the Court, this Suit is Continued till next Court for the Deft.

On Petition for £1.13.3 sd. to be due by Acct. - George Blake, Pltf. VS William Moore, Deft., this day came the Pltf. by his attorney and the Deft. not appearing, it is considered by the Court that the Pltf. recover against the sd. Deft., £1, 13 shillings, 3 pence together with his cost by him abt. this Suit expended.

Page 38

On Petition - Samuel Earnest[?], Pltf. VS Ralph Wormeley, Esqr., Deft., on the motion of the sd. Pltf. by his attorney it is ordered that this suit be dismissed and the Deft to pay the costs.

Ordered that George Blake pay John Hibble for seven days attendance as witness at this Court according to Law.

Absent – Overton Cosby, Gent.

On the motion of Overton Cosby, Letters of Admin. is granted him on the Estate of Samuel Wortham, he having taken the Oath of Admin. and entered into Bond according to Law.

In Chancery - Overton Cosby & James Ross acting of the last Will & Testament of James Mills, Esqr., dec'd., Pltf. agst. William Elliot, of the last will & testament of Elizabeth Elliot, dec'd, Deft. The Deft. having stood out all process of contempt & failing to appear and answer the Pltf. Bill. On the Motion of the sd. Pltf. by their Counsel, their bill is take for confessed and there upon it is Decreed & Ordered that the Deft. be henceforth barred and foreclosed of and from all equity of redemption in and to the mortgaged premises containing 550 a. of land and the water Grist Mill & slaves & personal chattels comprised in the deed of Mortgage mentioned and referred to in the Pltf. bill. That the Pltf. make sale of the sd. lands, mill, **slaves** and personal chattels to the highest bidder for ready money giving at least 10 days public notice of the time and place of such sale. That upon such sale of lands and mill afsd. or of any part thereof, the sd. Deft. do join with the Pltf. in making & executing such Deed or Deeds in the Law as shall be sufficient for passing and conveying the fee simple Estate thereon unto the purchaser or purchasers thereof, that the Pltf. do apply the money wch. may arise from the sd. Sales first in discharge of the Debt mentioned in the sd. Mortgage amounting to £245, 14 shillings, 1 penny and lawful interest thereon from 28 Jul 1772 to the time of sale, next in discharge of the debt due to James Mills & Co. amounting to £9, 5 shillings, 2 pence farthing with lawful interest thereon from 15 Feb 1775 to the time of payment and lastly the surcharge of the money of any arising from sd. Sales be paid unto the Deft. and the Deft. pay unto the Pltf. their costs.

Present – John George & Overton Cosby, Gent.

The Division of the Slaves devised to Edmund Mickelburrough's children by Henry Mickelburrough, dec'd., returned and Ordered to be Recorded.

Virginia – At a General Court held in Richmond, 26 April 1783, on the motion if William Webb, of the Orange County, who made Oath and together with Jacob Smith, of Henrico Co., and William Quarles of Spotsylvania Co., entered into and ackn.d their Bond in the penalty of £5,000, Condition as the Law directs, Certificate is granted him for obtaining Letters of Administration on the Estate of Henry Thacker, dec'd, in due form.

In Chancery – William Webb, Pltf. VS Samuel Klug, Clerk Admin. of George Lorimer, dec'd. The Bill and Answer being read and duly considered by the Court, it is Decreed that the Pltf. recover of the

42

Defendant, the Slaves in the bill mentioned, to wit: Anthony, [continued on next page]

Page 39

Betty, Mary, Isaac, Johnny, Nanny (Chitty when found the sd. Chitty it is supposed being gone to the English) and also £196 for the hire of the sd. Negroes to this time and that the Deft. pay the Pltf. his costs.

Absent – John George, Gent.

Ordered that Sinah, a Negro woman belonging to Daniel Dejarnatt be set county Levy free.

Absent – George Daniel, Gent.

In Case - Philip Gulley, Pltf., VS George Daniel & of Beverley Daniel, dec'd, Deft., came the Pltf. by his attorney as the Deft. by their attorney and the sd. Deft. prey and have leave to Imparle here till the next and then to plead.

In Debt – Nelson Daniel, Pltf., VS Betty Kemp, Deft., By consent of parties this Suit is referred to Benjamin Dabney and his award to be the judgment of the Court.

In Debt - Robert Ware, Senr., Pltf., VS John Thurston & Roberton, Deft., the Deft. John being arrested and not appearing tho Solemnly called, on the motion of the sd. Pltf by his attorney, it is Ordered that Judgment be entered against the Deft. John and George Bird, Gent., Sheriff for the Debt in the declaration mentioned unless the sd. Deft. shall at the next Court give Special bail and plead to Issue, this Suit abates as to Robert the other Deft. by his death.

In Case - William Churchill, Pltf. VS Benjamin Churchill, of Hannah Churchill, dec'd, Came as well the Pltf. by his attorney as the Deft. by his attorney, and the sd. Deft. prays and has have to Imparle here till the next Court and then to plead.

In Debt – George Daniel, of Beverley Daniel, dec'd, Pltf. VS Charles Read, Deft., the Deft. being arrested and not appearing tho Solemnly called, on the motion of the sd. Pltf by his attorney, it is Ordered that Judgment be entered against the Deft. for the Debt in the declaration mentioned unless the sd. Deft. shall at the next Court give Special bail and plead to Issue

Absent – Overton Cosby, Gent.

In Case - James Mills & Co., Pltf. VS Griffin Tuggle, Deft., This day came the parties by their attorneys and thereupon came also a Jury to wit. John Quarles Francis Ross, Wilkinson Barzey, William George, Harry Beverley Yates, Nicholas Tuggle, Henry Chowning, James Lee, William Roane, Lawrence Meacham, Daniel Dejarnatt, John Brooks, who being elected tried and sworn upon the issue joined, upon their Oaths that the Deft. did assume upon himself the manner and form, as the sd. Pltf. against him hath declared and they do asses the sd. Pltf. damages by occasion of the not[?] performance of that assumption, to £19, 8 shillings, 2 pence, half-penny [can't read] his costs. Them for it is considered by the Court that the sd. Pltf. [can't read] in form afsd., assessed [continued on next page]

Page 40

[continued from previous page] and his costs by him abt. this Suit on his behalf expended and the Deft. in Mercy, etc.

On Petition - William Kidd, Pltf. VS Lawrence Meacham, Deft., for £3, 5 shillings by note under the hand of the sd. Deft. as is set forth in the Petition, therefore it is considered by the Court that the Pltf. recover against the sd. Deft. £3, 5 shillings together with his Costs abt. this Suit expended.

On Petition - Thomas Courtney, Pltf., VS John Layton, Deft., for reasons appearing to the Court, this Suit is continued till next Court for the Deft.

On the motion of William Kidd his Ordinary license is renewed.

Present – Maurice Smith. Absent – Overton Cosby, Gent.

On Petition for £1.14.9, said to be due by account - Rhoda Taylor, Pltf., VS Charles Reade, Deft., this day came the Pltf. by his attorney & the Deft. not appearing it is considered by the Court that the Pltf. recover against the Deft. £1, 14 shillings, 9 pence together with his costs abt. the Suit expended.

On Petition - John George, Junr., Pltf., VS John Montague, of James Montague, Deft., the sd. Deft. not being arrested on alias Petition on the motion of the Pltf. is granted him.

On Petition - John George, Junr., Pltf., VS Harry Beverley Yates, Deft., for 300 lbs. net Pork by note under the hand of the sd. Deft. as set forth in the Petition, therefore it is considered by the Court that the Pltf. recover against the Deft. 300 lbs. net Pork at 30/ & 6 together with his costs abt. this suit expended.

In Debt - John Hodges assignee of Charles Grymes, Pltf., VS William Murray, came the Pltf. by his attorney and Thomas Moore comes in to Court and

44

undertakes that if the sd. Deft. shall be cast in the action, he will pay the costs and condemnation of the Court, or render his body to prison in Execution for the same , of the he the said Thomas Moore his attorney prays and has leave to Imparle here till the next Court and thereto plead.

Present – George Daniel. Absent – James Ross, Gent.

Page 41

Absent – Maurice Smith. Present – Overton Cosby, Gent.

In Debt – Benjamin Hackney, Pltf., VS John Smith & William George, Deft., the Deft. being arrested and not appearing tho Solemnly called, on the motion of the sd. Pltf by his attorney, it is Ordered that Judgment be entered against the Deft., and for their common bail for the Debt in the declaration mentioned unless the sd. Deft. shall at the next Court give Special bail and plead to Issue.

In Debt – William Murray, Pltf., VS John Smith, Deft., this Suit is dismissed at the Deft. costs.

In Debt - Thomas Sanders, Pltf. VS Isaac Digges, Deft., the Deft. being arrested and not appearing tho Solemnly called, on the motion of the sd. Pltf by his attorney, it is Ordered that Judgment be entered against the Deft. and William Elliot, his bail, for the Debt in the declaration mentioned unless the sd. Deft. shall at the next Court give Special bail and plead to Issue

In Debt – Charles Grymes, Pltf., VS William Dame, Admin. of John Dance, Deft., this Suit is dismissed at the Deft. costs.

[No case of Pltf. or Deft. or case type noted, just the following] the Deft. being arrested and not appearing tho Solemnly called, on the motion of the sd. Pltf by his attorney, it is Ordered that Judgment be entered against the Deft. for the Debt in the declaration mentioned unless the sd. Deft. shall at the next Court give Special bail and plead to Issue

In Case - Francis Ross, Pltf. VS Charles Grymes, Deft. , came the Pltf. by his attorney as the Deft by his attorney and the sd. Deft. prays and has have to Imparle here till the next Court and then to plead.

Deed of Gift from Charles Grymes to William Row[?] Dance was ackn.d by the sd. Grymes and Ordered to be Recorded.

By Summons – continued till next Court - Edmund Berkeley & Gentlemen Justices, Pltf. VS Thomas Segar, Gent., Deft.

In Case - Henry Vass, Gent., Pltf. VS Benjamin Sewards, Deft., by order of the Pltf. this Suit dismissed.

In Case - George Daniel Exec of Beverley Daniel, dec'd, Pltf. VS Thomas Taff, Deft. [continued on next page]

Page 42

The Deft. not being arrested on the motion of th sd. Pltf. by Benjamin Dabney their attorney an attachment is awarded the sd. Pltf. against the Deft. for £50 and costs returnable here at the next Court.

In Debt - Francis Cloudas & Richard Street, of William Cloudas, dec'd, Pltf., VS John Thurston & James Lee, Deft., the Suit is dismissed by Order of the Pltf.

In Case - James Quarles, of John Quarles, dec'd, Pltf. VS John Pond Coton, Admin. of William Parry, dec'd, Deft., for reasons appearing the Court Suit is dismissed.

In Case – Dudley Vaughan, Pltf. VS William Churchill, Deft., Came as well the Pltf. by his attorney as the Deft. by his attorney and the sd. Deft. prays and has leave to Imparle here till next Court and then to plead.

In Debt. - John Miller, of Christopher Miller, dec'd, Pltf. VS Mary Berry & Isaac Jones, Deft., this Suit abates by the death of the Deft.

In Case - Andrew Davis, Pltf., VS William Jackson, Deft., this Suit is continued till next Court.

In Case – Samuel Drummond, Pltf. VS Hugh Walker, Deft., came the parties by their attorneys and the sd. Deft. defends the force & Injury when [can't read] and sd. that he did not undertake in manner & form as the Pltf. against him hath declared, and the sd. Deft. further sayeth that he did not at any time within five years bef. the day the Pltf suing out the sd. original Writ, assume upon himself in manner & form as the Pltf. above complains against him and the Pltf. replies that the Deft. did undertake within five years bef. as in manner & form as the Pltf. hath declared against him and this he prays may be inquired into by the County and the Deft. prays likewise the same, therefore the trial of Issues is referred till the next Court.

In Case - Hugh Walker, Pltf. VS John Hughes, Deft., Came the parties by their attorneys and the sd. Deft. defends the force & inquiry when [can't read] and saith that he did not undertake in manner and form as the Pltf. against him hath declared and of this he puts himself upon his Country & the Pltf. likewise, etc. and therefore the trial of Issues is referred till the next Court.

Absent – George Daniel. Present – Thomas Segar, Gent.

Page 43

In Case - Edmund Pendleton and Peter Lyons, Admin. of John Robinson, Esqr., dec'd, Pltf. VS Samuel Daniel, Deft, The Sheriff having Returned that he had attached Book the Estate of the sd. Deft. and the sd. Deft. appearing tho Solemnly called on the motion f the sd. Pltf. by his attorney. It is considered by the Court that the sd. Pltf. recover against the sd. Deft. £14, 2 pence being the Debt in the Declaration mentioned and their costs abt. this suit in this behalf expended and the sd. Deft. in [can't read] ordered that Attached effects be released.

In Case - Edmund Pendleton and Peter Lyons, Admin. of John Robinson, Esqr., dec'd, Pltf. VS Robert Daniel & John Jackson, of George Davis, Deft., came the parties by their attorneys and the sd. Deft. Jackson defends the force & Injury to and saith that he did not undertake in manner & form as the Pltf. against him declares and of this he puts himself upon his Country & sd. Pltf. likewise, etc., therefore the trial of Issues is referred till the next Court, the Suit abates as to the other Deft. by his death.

In Debt - Edward & James Ware, of Edward Ware, dec'd, Pltf. VS James Mountague, Deft., the Suit abates by the Deft.'s death.

In Case – Ordered that Ralph Wormeley by summoned to appear at the next Court to declare whether he will qualify as an to the Will of Christopher Robinson, dec'd.

In Case - Archibald Mc Call, Pltf. VS John Bream, Admin, of John Bream, dec'd, the Deft. being arrested and not appearing tho Solemnly called, on the motion of the sd. Pltf by his attorney, it is Ordered that Judgment be entered against him for the Debt in the declaration mentioned unless the sd. Deft. shall at the next Court give Special bail and plead to Issue

In Debt - John & George Fowlers, Pltf. VS Reuben Shelton, Deft., this Suit is continued till next Court for the Deft.

In Debt - Maurice Smith & Philip Montague, of William Roane, dec'd, Pltf. VS John Kidd, Deft., this suit abates by the Deft.'s death.

In Debt - John & George Fowlers, Pltf. VS John Cornelius, Deft., this Suit abates by the death of Deft.

In Debt - John Miller, of Christopher, Miller, dec'd, Pltf, VS Mary Berry & Isaac Jones, this Suit abates by the death of the Pltf.

Page 44

[Can't read] – Commonwealth, Pltf. VS George Dillard, Simon Laughlin, William Davis[?], Thomas Sanders, Deft., continued till next Court.

Present. of the Grand Jury dismissed - Commonwealth, Pltf. VS Overton Cosby, Deft.

Presentment of the Grand Jury - Commonwealth, Pltf. VS Ralph Watts, Daniel Stringer, Daniel Stringer[?], Samuel Brooks, George West[?], Deft., continued till next Court.

Presentment of the Grand Jury abates by the Deft.'s death – Commonwealth, Pltf. VS Reuben Allen, Deft.

Presentment of the Grand Jury abates by the Deft.'s death – Commonwealth, Pltf. VS John Brooks, Nancy Dudley, Sarah Parker, Thos. Healy, Deft.

Presentment of the Grand Jury – Commonwealth, Pltf. VS John Wake, Deft., this day came the Pltf. by Thomas Moore, his attorney, and the Deft. not appearing, it is considered by the Court that for the sd. offense he make his fine to the Commonwealth by the payment of 2,000 lbs. of tobacco and the costs.

Presentment of the Grand Jury – Commonwealth, Pltf., VS John Kibble, Deft. Came the parities by their attorneys and thereupon a jury to wit. Jonathan Denison, Francis Ross, Harry Beverley Yates, Nicholas Tuggle, Henry Chowning, Thomas Crittenden, Warner Blake, James Kidd, Thomas Stiff, Henry Batchelder, William George & Lawrence Meacham, who being elected, tried & sworn the truth to speak upon the Issue joined upon their Oaths doth say that the Deft. oweth nothing of the Debt in the Declaration mentioned, as in pleading is set forth, therefore it is considered by the Court that the Pltf. take nothing by his bill, but for the false claimour[?] by in [can't read], and that the Deft. go therefore home without day, etc. [sentence erased ?].

In Debt - William Churchill, Pltf. VS Charles Edwards, Deft., the suit is dismissed by Pltf. order.

Agrippa Dunn against Thomas Turner dismissed by the Court.

Ordered that the Court be adjourned till tomorrow 9 o'clock. The Minutes of this proceeding were signed by Edmund Berkeley, Gent.

At a Court held for Middlesex County at the Courthouse in Urbanna on Wedsday the 28th day of April 1784

Present – Edmund Berkeley, George Daniel, Overton Cosby, and James Ross, Gent.

Presentment of Grand Jury - Commonwealth, Pltf. VS George Lorimer, Deft., for reasons appearing to the Court the Suit is dismissed.

Tobacco inspected within twelve months as a Commutable is valued at 28 Shillings per hundred, Flour not inspected more than three months at 2 pence per pound & hemp at 25 shillings per hundred.

On Petition – James Campbell, Pltf. VS Lawrence Meacham, Deft., this suit is continued till next Court for the Deft.

On Petition - Simon Fraser, Pltf. VS Robert Curtis, Deft., this suit is dismissed.

On Petition - John and George Fowlers, Pltf. VS William Gest, Deft. By order under the hand and seal of the sd. Deft. for £4, 6 shillings, with legal interest thereon from the 22 Nov 1773, as is set forth in the Petition, therefore it is considered by the Court that the Pltf. recover against the sd. Deft. £4, 6 shillings, with legal interest together with their costs abt. the suit expended.

In Debt - Latan Mountague, Pltf. VS William Thurston, Deft., the Deft. being arrested and not appearing tho Solemnly called, on the motion of the sd. Pltf by his attorney, it is Ordered that Judgment be entered against the Deft. for the Debt in the declaration mentioned unless the sd. Deft. shall at the next Court give Special bail and plead to Issue

In Debt - James Mills & Co., Pltf. VS William Churchill, Deft., the Deft. came into Court and certified judgment therefore it is considered by the Court that the sd. Pltf. recover against the sd. Deft. £67, 5 shillings and 9 pence being the Deft in the declaration mentioned and their costs by them their Suit in the behalf expended and the sd. Deft. in Mercy, etc., but this Judgment is to be discharged by the payment of [nothing further].

In Debt - George Lorimer assignee of Benjamin [can't read] Pltf. VS Churchill Armistead and William Churchill, Deft., this suit abates by the death of the Pltf.

In Chancery - Andrew Davis, Pltf. VS Ralph Wormeley, William Churchill and Philip Ludwell Grymes, Trustees for the sale of Wm. Armistead's land, Deft., for reason appearing to the Court, this Suit is Continued till next Court.

On Scere Facias – Charles Myron Thurston, of Hugh Spotswood, Pltf., VS John Hedges, Deft., came as well the Pltf. by his attorney as the Deft by his attorney and the sd. Deft. craves Oyer of the sd. Writ, and to him it is granted till the next Court and then to Plead.

In Debt – John & George Fowlers, Pltf. VS Josiah Greenwood, Deft., abates by the Deft. death.

In Debt. Richard Corbin, Esqr. Pltf. VS William Churchill, Deft., the Deft. came into Court and confessed Judgment [several words crossed out] therefore it is considered by the Court that the Pltf. recover against the sd. Deft. £267, being the debt in the declaration mentioned and his costs by him abt. this suit in his behalf expended and the sd. Deft in mercy etc. But this Judgment is to be discharged by the payment of one hundred and _____ with legal interest for the ____ day of _____ one thousand seven hundred _____ till paid. Memorandum all just discounts are to be allowed the Deft.

On Petition for £2.8 - Hugh Walker, Pltf. VS Charles Alexander, Deft., this day the Deft. by his attorney and the deft not appearing, it is considered by the Court that the Pltf. recover against the Deft. £2.8 together with his costs abt. his Suit expended.

In Debt – Hugh Walker, Pltf., VS John Smith, of Augustine Smith, Deft., came the Pltf. as well as his attorney as the Deft by his attorney and the sd. Deft. prays and has leave to Imparle here till the next Court and then to plead.

Settlement of John Daniel's Estate is continued till next Court.

On Attachment , continued till next Court - David Loudon, Pltf. VS John Bagot, Deft., the Deft.

Page 47

George Bird, Pltf. VS Simon Fraser, Deft., came as well the Pltf. by his attorney as the Deft. by his attorney and the sd. Deft. prays and has have to Imparle here till the next Court and then to plead.

In Case - Richard Corbin, Esqr., Pltf., VS John Boughton, Deft., the Deft. not appearing though again tho Solemnly called on the motion of the sd. Pltf by his attorney, it is considered that Judgment that the Order of the last Court be confirmed and that the damages be ascertained by an Inquiry thereof by a Jury at the next Court.

Motion abates by Deft. death - Robert Spratt, Pltf. VS James Wortham, Deft.

In Debt - John Baker & James Holderness, of the Estate of Blake Baker, dec'd, Pltf. VS William Mason, Deft., the Deft. being arrested and not appearing tho Solemnly called, on the motion of the sd. Pltf by his attorney, it is Ordered that Judgment be entered against the Deft. for the Debt in the declaration mentioned unless the sd. Deft. shall at the next Court give Special bail and plead to Issue.

In Debt - Simon Fraser, Pltf. VS Charles Lee, Deft., the Deft. not appearing tho Solemnly called, on the motion of the sd. Pltf by his attorney, it is ordered that the Order of the last Court bee confirmed and the at the damages be ascertained upon an Inquiry thereof a Jury as the next Court.

In Case - John Hibble, Pltf. VS Daniel Stringer, Deft., the Deft. being arrested and not appearing tho Solemnly called, on the motion of the sd. Pltf by his attorney, it is Ordered that Judgment be entered against the Deft. for the Debt in the declaration mentioned unless the sd. Deft. shall at the next Court give Special bail and plead to Issue.

On Petition continued till next Court – Samuel Daniel, Pltf. VS Joseph Hardee, Deft.

In Case – Richard Barker, Pltf., VS David Loudon, Deft., the Deft not appearing tho Solemnly called, on the motion of the sd. Pltf by his attorney, it is considered that the Order of the last Court be confirmed and that the damages be ascertained upon an Inquiry thereof by a Jury at the next Court.

On an Indictment - The Commonwealth, Pltf. VS George Bush, Deft., came the parties by their attorneys and upon a Jury, to wit: Jonathan Denison, Francis Ross [continued on next page]

Page 48

Harry Beverley Yates, Nicholas Tuggle, Henry Chowning, Thomas Crittenden, Warner Blake, James Kidd, Henry Batchelder, William George, Lawrence Meacham, and William Roane[?], who being elected, tried & sworn the truth to speak upon the Issue joined upon their Oaths doth say that the Deft. owes to this Commonwealth £10 besides its costs, therefore it is considered by the Court that the sd. Pltf. recover against the sd. Deft. its damages afsd. in form afsd. assessed and its costs abt. the Suit in this behalf as pleaded, and the sd. Deft. in Mercy, etc.

An Attachment continued till next Court - Benjamin William, Pltf. VS Richard Bird, Deft.

In Case abates by Deft.'s death – Samuel Daniel, Pltf. VS James Wortham, Deft.

In Case - John Jackson, Pltf. VS George Warwick & James Mc Han, Deft., came the Pltf. by his Attorney and the Deft, by his Attorney and on motion of the sd. Deft., the Order of the last Court is set aside and the sd. Deft prays and have leave to Imparle here till the next Court and then to plead.

Dee Poll from Ralph Wormeley, Esqr. to Thomas Blake proved by the Oaths of the witnesses thereto and Ordered to be Recorded.

In Case - Benjamin Williams, Pltf. VS Mary Haddon & Robert Aldrige, of Thos. Haddon, Deft., this Suit abates as to Mary Haddon by her death and by return as to Robert Aldrige.

In Case - Elizabeth Ann Segar by Thomas Segar their Guardian and next Friend, Pltf. VS John Wake, Deft., the Deft. being arrested and not appearing tho Solemnly called, on the motion of the sd. Pltf by his attorney, it is Ordered that Judgment be entered against the Deft. for the Debt in the declaration mentioned unless the sd. Deft. shall at the next Court give Special bail and plead to Issue.

In Debt - James Wortham, Admin. of Samuel Wortham, dec'd, Pltf. VS Joseph Hardee & others, this suit abates by Pltf.'s death.

In Debt – Dismissed by [can't read] Order - William Churchill, Pltf. VS Johnston Wake, Deft.

Page 49

In Debt - William Churchill, who as well for the Commonwealth, as for himself, Pltf. VS Robert Wake, Deft., came the parties by their attorneys and upon a Jury, to wit: Jonathan Denison, Francis Ross, Harry Beverley Yates, Nicholas Tuggle, Henry Chowning, Thomas Crittenden, Warner Blake, James Kidd, Henry Batchelder, William George, Lawrence Meacham, and William Roane, who being elected, tried & sworn the truth to speak upon the Issue joined upon their Oaths doth say that the Deft. owes to the Commonwealth 500 lbs. of tobacco and their costs, therefore it is considered by the Court, that the sd. Pltf. recover against the Deft. their damages afsd. in form afsd. assessed and their costs abt. their suit in their behalf expended, and the sd. Deft. in mercy, etc.

In Case dismissed by Pltf. Order - John Jackson, Pltf. VS John Healy, Deft.

In Case - In Case - Churchill Blakey, Pltf. VS Charles Lee, Deft., the Deft. being arrested and not appearing tho Solemnly called, on the motion of the sd. Pltf by his attorney, it is Ordered that Judgment be entered against the Deft. for the Debt in the declaration mentioned unless the sd. Deft. shall appear at the next Court give Special bail and plead to Issue.

John Tarpley, Pltf., VS Thomas Taff, Deft., came as well the Pltf. by his attorney as the Deft. by his attorney and the sd. Deft. prays and have leave to Imparle till the next Court and then to plead.

In Case dismissed by Pltf. Order - William Pryor, Pltf. VS John Healy & George Dunlevy, Deft.

For assault & battery - Lawrence Meacham, Pltf., VS William Harvey, Deft., this Suit by the consent of the parties is dismissed and ordered that the Deft pay unto the Pltf. his costs.

On Petition continued till next Court - John Dean, Pltf. VS William Hackney, Deft.

In Case - Henry Vass, Pltf. VS Jonathan Eyre, Deft., the Deft. appearing tho solemnly called on the motion of the sd. Deft by his attorney, it is ordered that the order of the last Court be confirmed and that the damages by ascertained upon an Inquiry thereof by a Jury at the next Court.

Page 50

In Debt – Commonwealth, Pltf. VS William Stiff, Deft., came the Pltf. by Thomas Moore, his attorney, and thereupon the Jury to wit: Jonathan Denison, Francis Ross, Harry Beverley Yates, Nicholas Tuggle, Henry Chowning, Thomas Crittenden, Warner Blake, James Kidd, Henry Batchelder, William George, Lawrence Meacham, and William Roane, who being elected, tried & sworn the truth to speak upon the Issue joined upon their Oaths doth say that the sd. Deft. owes to the Commonwealth £4,3 shillings, 4 pence, therefore it is considered by the Court, that the sd. Pltf. recover against the Deft. damages afsd. in form afsd. assessed and its costs abt. its Suit in this behalf expended & the sd. Deft. in mercy , etc.

In Debt this Suit is dismissed – Commonwealth, Pltf. VS John Wake, Deft.

In Debt. this Suit is dismissed - Commonwealth, Pltf. VS Elizabeth Jackson, Deft.

In Case abates by the Deft. death - William Churchill, Pltf. VS George Lorimer, Deft.

In Case abates by Deft. Death - George Lorimer, Pltf. VS John Wortham, Deft.

In Debt – Thomas Moore, who as well for the Commonwealth, as for himself, Pltf. VS David Powell, Deft., came the Pltf. by Thomas Moore, his attorney, and thereupon the Jury to wit: Jonathan Denison, Francis Ross, Harry Beverley Yates, Nicholas Tuggle, Henry Chowning, Thomas Crittenden, Warner Blake, James Kidd, Henry Batchelder, William George, Lawrence Meacham, and William Roane, who being elected, tried & sworn the truth to speak upon the Issue joined upon their Oaths doth say that the sd. Deft. owes to the Pltf. £2,15 shillings, 6 pence, therefore it is considered by the Court, that the sd. Pltf. recover against the Deft. their damages afsd. in form afsd. assessed and their costs abt. its Suit in this behalf expended & the sd. Deft. in mercy , etc.

In Debt – Thomas Moore, who as well for the Commonwealth, as for himself, Pltf. VS Robert Wake, Deft., came the Pltf. their attorney, and thereupon the Jury to wit: Jonathan Denison, Francis Ross, Harry Beverley Yates, Nicholas Tuggle, Henry Chowning, Thomas Crittenden, Warner Blake, James Kidd, Henry Batchelder, William George, Lawrence Meacham, and William Roane, who being elected, tried & sworn the truth to speak upon the Issue joined upon their Oaths doth say that the sd. Deft. owes to the Pltf. £2,15 shillings, 6 pence, half penny, therefore it is considered by the Court, that the sd. Pltf. recover against the Deft. their damages afsd. in form afsd. assessed and their costs abt. its Suit in this behalf expended & the sd. Deft. in mercy , etc.

Page 51

In Debt – Same, Pltf. VS Johnston Wake, Deft., the Deft not being arrested and not appearing tho Solemnly called on the motion of the sd. Pltf. by his attorney, an alias Capias is granted him returnable to the next Court.

In Debt – Same, Pltf. VS John Wake, Deft., the Deft not being arrested and not appearing tho Solemnly called on the motion of the sd. Pltf. by his attorney, an attachment is awarded the sd. Pltf. against the sd. Deft., returnable here at the next Court.

In Debt – Same, Pltf. VS George Jackson, Deft., the Deft not being arrested and not appearing tho Solemnly called on the motion of the sd. Pltf. by his attorney, an attachment is awarded the sd. Pltf. against the sd. Deft., returnable here at the next Court.

In Debt – Same, Pltf. VS John Jackson, Deft., came the Pltf. their attorney, and thereupon the Jury to wit: Jonathan Denison, Francis Ross, Harry Beverley Yates, Nicholas Tuggle, Henry Chowning, Thomas Crittenden, Warner Blake, James Kidd, Henry Batchelder, William George, Lawrence Meacham, and

William Roane, who being elected, tried & sworn the truth to speak upon the
Issue joined upon their Oaths doth say that the sd. Deft. owes to the Pltf. £2,15
shillings, 6 pence, half penny, therefore it is considered by the Court, that the
sd. Pltf. recover against the Deft. their damages afsd. in form afsd. assessed and
their costs abt. its Suit in this behalf expended & the sd. Deft. in mercy , etc.

In Debt – Same, Pltf. VS William Jackson, Deft., came the Pltf. their attorney,
and thereupon the Jury to wit: Jonathan Denison, Francis Ross, Harry Beverley
Yates, Nicholas Tuggle, Henry Chowning, Thomas Crittenden, Warner Blake,
James Kidd, Henry Batchelder, William George, Lawrence Meacham, and
William Roane, who being elected, tried & sworn the truth to speak upon the
Issue joined upon their Oaths doth say that the sd. Deft. owes to the Pltf. £2,15
shillings, 6 pence, half penny, therefore it is considered by the Court, that the
sd. Pltf. recover against the Deft. their damages afsd. in form afsd. assessed and
their costs abt. its Suit in this behalf expended & the sd. Deft. in mercy , etc.

In Debt – Same, Pltf. VS William Boss, Deft., came the Pltf. their attorney, and
thereupon the Jury to wit: Jonathan Denison, Francis Ross, Harry Beverley
Yates, Nicholas Tuggle, Henry Chowning, Thomas Crittenden, Warner Blake,
James Kidd, Henry Batchelder, William George, Lawrence Meacham, and
William Roane, who being elected, tried & sworn the truth to speak upon the
Issue joined upon their Oaths doth say that the sd. Deft. owes to the Pltf. £2,15
shillings, 6 pence, half penny, therefore it is considered by the Court, that the
sd. Pltf. recover against the Deft. their damages afsd. in form afsd. assessed and
their costs abt. its Suit in this behalf expended & the sd. Deft. in mercy , etc.

Page 52

In Debt – Thomas Moore, who as well for the Commonwealth, as for himself,
Pltf. VS John Boss, Deft., came the Pltf. their attorney, and thereupon the Jury to
wit: Jonathan Denison, Francis Ross, Harry Beverley Yates, Nicholas Tuggle,
Henry Chowning, Thomas Crittenden, Warner Blake, James Kidd, Henry
Batchelder, William George, Lawrence Meacham, and William Roane, who
being elected, tried & sworn the truth to speak upon the Issue joined upon their
Oaths doth say that the sd. Deft. owes to the Pltf. £2,15 shillings, 6 pence, half
penny, therefore it is considered by the Court, that the sd. Pltf. recover against
the Deft. their damages afsd. in form afsd. assessed and their costs abt. its Suit in
this behalf expended & the sd. Deft. in mercy , etc.

In Debt – Same, Pltf. VS Ann Wilcocks, Deft., came the Pltf. their attorney, and
thereupon the Jury to wit: Jonathan Denison, Francis Ross, Harry Beverley
Yates, Nicholas Tuggle, Henry Chowning, Thomas Crittenden, Warner Blake,
James Kidd, Henry Batchelder, William George, Lawrence Meacham, and
William Roane, who being elected, tried & sworn the truth to speak upon the
Issue joined upon their Oaths doth say that the sd. Deft. owes to the Pltf. £2,15

shillings, 6 pence, half penny, therefore it is considered by the Court, that the sd. Pltf. recover against the Deft. their damages afsd. in form afsd. assessed and their costs abt. its Suit in this behalf expended & the sd. Deft. in mercy , etc.

In Debt dismissed by Pltf. Order – Same, Pltf. VS George Bush.

In Debt – Same, Pltf. VS Thomas Blake, Junr., the Deft. not being arrested and not appearing tho Solemnly called on the motion of the sd. Pltf. by their attorney, attachment is awarded them against the sd. Deft, returnable here at next Court.

In Debt – Same, Pltf. VS George Blake, the Deft. not being arrested and not appearing tho Solemnly called on the motion of the sd. Pltf. by their attorney, attachment is awarded them against the sd. Deft, returnable here at next Court.

In Debt – Same, Pltf. VS Thomas Edwards, Deft., came the Pltf. their attorney, and thereupon the Jury to wit: Jonathan Denison, Francis Ross, Harry Beverley Yates, Nicholas Tuggle, Henry Chowning, Thomas Crittenden, Warner Blake, James Kidd, Henry Batchelder, William George, Lawrence Meacham, and William Roane, who being elected, tried & sworn the truth to speak upon the Issue joined upon their Oaths doth say that the sd. Deft. owes to the Pltf. £2,15 shillings, 6 pence, half penny, therefore it is considered by the Court, that the sd. Pltf. recover against the Deft. their damages afsd. in form afsd. assessed and their costs abt. its Suit in this behalf expended & the sd. Deft. in mercy , etc.

Page 53

In Debt - Same, Pltf. VS William Stiff, Deft., came the Pltf. their attorney, and thereupon the Jury to wit: Jonathan Denison, Francis Ross, Harry Beverley Yates, Nicholas Tuggle, Henry Chowning, Thomas Crittenden, Warner Blake, James Kidd, Henry Batchelder, William George, Lawrence Meacham, and William Roane, who being elected, tried & sworn the truth to speak upon the Issue joined upon their Oaths doth say that the sd. Deft. owes to the Pltf. £2,15 shillings, 6 pence, half penny, therefore it is considered by the Court, that the sd. Pltf. recover against the Deft. their damages afsd. in form afsd. assessed and their costs abt. its Suit in this behalf expended & the sd. Deft. in mercy , etc.

In Debt – dismissed by Pltf. Order – William Churchill, Pltf. VS Anderson Miller, Deft.

Absent – Edmund Berkeley, Present- George Daniel, Gent.

In Case – Jack Gardner, Pltf, VS John Meacham, Deft., the Deft being arrested and not appearing tho Solemnly called on the motion of the sd. Pltf. by their attorney, it is Ordered that Judgment be entered against the Deft. for the Debt in the declaration mentioned unless the sd. Deft shall appear at next Court, given Special bail and plead to Issue.

In Case - William Hakney[Hackney?], Pltf. VS Thomas Sanders, Deft., came as well the Pltf by attorney as the Deft by his attorney and the sd. Deft prays and has leave to Imparle here till the next Court and then to plead.

By Attachment, continued till next Court - Jonathan Eyre, Pltf. VS Joseph Hardee, Deft.

In Debt – abates by the Deft. death - Jack Gardner, Assignee. of Edward Didlake, Pltf. VS Robert Thurston

In Case dismiss, Deft. to pay costs – Ann Wood, Pltf. VS John George, Junr, Deft.

In Case - James Lee, Pltf. VS Ralph Watts, came as well the Pltf. by his attorney and the sd. Deft. defends the same and injury when, etc. and saith that he did not [can't read] upon himself in manner form as the Pltf. complains against him, and of this he puts himself upon his Country and the Pltf likewise therefore the trial of the issue is referred till the next Court.

In Case an process ordered – Betty Sanders, Pltf. VS Benjamin Hackney, Deft.

Page 54

In Case non [can't read - John Jackson, Junr., Pltf. VS Robert Mc Tyre, Deft.

In Case - Alexander Anderson, Pltf. VS John Boss, Deft., came as well the Pltf by attorney as the Deft by his attorney and the sd. Deft prays and has leave to Imparle here till the next Court and then to plead.

William Hill, Pltf. VS Alexander Anderson, Deft., came as well the Pltf by attorney as the Deft by his attorney and the sd. Deft prays and has have to Imparle here till the next Court and then to plead.

Ejectment – Charles Thurston Lessee of Philp Edmondson, Pltf., VS William Holdfast, Deft., by consent of parties this Suit is dismissed.

In Case – Isaac Degges, Pltf. VS Hugh Walker, Deft., came as well the Pltf by attorney as the Deft by his attorney and the sd. Deft prays and has have to Imparle here till the next Court and then to plead.

In Chancery – Daniel Dejarnatt, Pltf. VS Robert Daniel & John Jackson, of George Davis, dec'd, Deft., tis Suit is continued till next Court for Bill.

In Case – William Murray, Pltf. VS Daniel Dejarnatt, Deft., continued by consent of parties till next Court.

In Chancery - Catharine Rivers[?], Admin. of Joseph Rivers, dec'd, Pltf. VS Hugh Walker, by consent this Suit is dismissed.

By Summons - The Justices, Pltf. VS Joseph Hardee, Deft., the Deft not being arrested and not appearing tho solemnly called on the motion of the sd. Pltf. by their attorney, attachment is awarded them returnable here at the next Court against the sd. Deft.

Page 55

In Case this Suit is dismissed by Pltf. Order – John Boss, Pltf. VS Johnston Wake, Deft.

In Case - Thomas Sanders, Pltf. VS Charles Edwards, Deft., came as well the Pltf. by his attorney and the sd. Deft. by his attorney and the sd. Deft. defends the force and injury when, etc. and saith that he did not assume upon himself in manner form following as the Pltf. above complains against him, and of this he puts himself upon his Country and the Pltf likewise therefore the trial of the issue is referred till the next Court.

In Case abates by Pltf. death - Robert Thurston, Pltf. VS Joseph Hardee, Deft.

In Case abates by Pltf. death - Robert Thurston, Pltf. VS Joseph Hardee, Deft.

In Case – Edward Didlake, Pltf., VS Daniel Dejarnatt, Deft., came as well the Pltf. by his attorney and the sd. Deft. by his attorney and the sd. Deft. defends the force and injury when, etc. and saith that he did not assume upon himself in manner form following as the Pltf. above complains against him, and of this he puts himself upon his Country and the Pltf likewise therefore the trial of the issue is referred till the next Court.

On Petition for £2.17.8 – Robert Spratt, Pltf. VS William Moore, Deft., came as well the Pltf. by his attorney and the sd. Deft. not appearing it is considered by the Court that the Pltf. recover against the Deft. £2, 17 shillings together with his costs abt. the Suit expended.

Ordered that George Daniel, Maurice Smith, William Murray, Gent., and Benjamin Bristow, or any three of them being first sworn bef. some Justice of the Peace for this County, do appraise the Estate of Samuel Wortham, dec'd in the hands of James Wortham and make their report to the next Court.

58

In Case - Joanna Curtis, Pltf. VS William Gest, Deft, The Deft not appearing tho Solemnly called on the motion of the sd. Pltf. by his attorney, it is considered that the order of the last Court be confirmed and that the damages be ascertained by an Inquiry thereof by a Jury at the next Court.

In Case abates by the Deft. death - William Elliott, Pltf. VS James Wortham, Deft.

Page 56

Justices against Mary [?] Blackburn survivors continued till next

In Case abates by Deft. death - Edward Conner, Pltf., VS George Lorimer, Deft.

In Case – Isaac Degges, Pltf. VS William Moore, Deft., the sd. Pltf. being arrested and not appearing tho Solemnly called on the motion of the sd. Pltf. by his attorney, it is considered that Judgment be entered against the Deft. for the Debt in the declaration mentioned unless the sd. Deft. shall appear at the next Court give Special back and plead to issue.

For Assault & Battery – Thomas Gains, Pltf. VS John Hunt, Deft., The Deft. not being arrested and appearing tho Solemnly called on the motion of the sd. Pltf. by his attorney and Alias Capias is awarded him against the sd. Deft. returnable here at next Court.

In Case abates by the Deft. death - Mary Bird, Pltf. VS George Lorimer, Deft.,

In Case abates by the deft. death - Mary Bird, Exec of Mary Hadden, dec'd, Pltf. VS George Lorimer, Deft..

On Petition for four barrels of corn - William Jones, Pltf. VS William Elliott, Deft., this day came the Pltf. by his attorney and the sd. Deft. not appearing it is considered by the Court that the Pltf. recover against the Deft. four barrels of corn together with his Costs abt. his Suit in his behalf expended.

On Petition contained till next Court by consent of parties - James Crosfield, Pltf., VS John Jossee, Deft.

In Debt dismissed by Pltf. Order in two actions – William Churchill, Pltf. VS John Wake, Deft.

In Debt - John Hughes, assignee of William Clayton, of John Clayton, Pltf. VS John Robinson, of Augustus Curtis, Deft., came as well the Pltf. by his attorney as the Deft by his attorney and the sd. Deft defends the force and injury when etc., and saith that the sd. Augustus Curtis in his lifetime paid the Debt in the

declaration mentioned according to the writing obligation therein also
[continued next page]

Page 57

[continued from previous page] mentioned and of this he puts himself upon the
Country and the Pltf. does likewise the same therefore the trial of the issue is
referred till the next Court.

In debt abates by the Deft. death - Edward Spencer, Pltf., VS Robert Thurston,
Deft.

In Debt - Robert Green assignee of Thomas Wilkie, Pltf. VS William Elliott,
Pltf., the Deft not being arrested & not appearing tho Solemnly called on the
motion of the sd. Pltf. by his attorney and Alias Capias is awarded him
returnable here at next Court.

William Dudley & Henry Fleet, of Edwin Fleet, Pltf. VS Joseph Hardee, Deft.,
the Deft being arrested and not appearing tho Solemnly called on the motion of
the sd. Pltf. by his attorney attachment is awarded them against the sd. Deft.
returnable here at next Court.

In Debt continued till next Court - John Humphris, Pltf., VS Elizabeth and
William Hackney, Deft.

In Debt - William Dudley & Henry Fleet, of Edwin Fleet, of William Fleet,
Pltf. VS William Gest, Deft., the Deft being arrested and not appearing tho
Solemnly called on the motion of the sd. Pltf. by his attorney, it is ordered that
Judgment be entered against the sd. Deft. for the Debt in the declaration
mentioned unless the sd. Deft. shall appear at the next Court given special bail
and plead to Issue.

In Debt - William Dudley & Henry Fleet, of Edwin Fleet, of William Fleet,
Pltf. VS Aggy Holden, Deft., the Deft being arrested and not appearing tho
Solemnly called on the motion of the sd. Pltf. by his attorney, it is ordered that
Judgment be entered against the sd. Deft. for the Debt in the declaration
mentioned unless the sd. Deft. shall appear at the next Court given special bail
and plead to Issue.

In Case abates by Pltf. death – John Throckmorton, Pltf. VS Lawrence
Meacham, Deft.

In Case - George Green, Pltf. VS John Curtis, Deft., came as well the Pltf. by his
attorney as the Deft. by his attorney and the sd. Deft. prays and has leave to
Imparle here till the next Court and then to plead.

60

In Debt abates by Pltf. death – George Lorimer, Pltf. VS John Montague, of James Montague, Deft.

Page 58

In Chancery – Alexander Anderson and Nanny, his wife, Thomas Scott, John Scott, Esther Scott and Elizabeth Scott, Complt. VS Nancy Scott and infant by Sally Scott, her Guardian, Deft., the Complt. having filed their bill time is granted till the next Court to answer the same.

In Case – John Layton, Pltf. VS George Pasquett, Deft., came as well the Pltf. by his attorney as the Deft by his attorney and on the motion of the sd. Deft., the Order of the last Court is set aside and the sd. Deft. prays and has leave to Imparle here till the next Court and then to plead.

In case - James Gregorie & George Lorimer, of John Daniel, dec'd, Pltf. VS Samuel Chowning, this suit is continued till next Court by consent of parties.

In Case - William Mountague, Pltf., VS Samuel Chowning, Deft., continued till next Court by consent of parties.

In Case – Edmund Pendleton & Peter Lyons, Admins. of John Robinson, Esqr., Pltf, VS Christopher Robinson, Deft., came as well the Pltf. by their attorney as the Deft. by his attorney and the sd. Deft. prays and has leave to to Imparle here till the next Court and then to plead.

In Chancery - Thomas Iveson, and infant by John King, his Guardian, Complt. VS Jane and Sally Morgan, co-heirs of John Morgan and James Gregorie, Deft., continued till next Court for report.

In Chancery till next Court - Simon Laughlin, Complt., VS Ann Tomkins, Deft.

In Chancery till next Court - Simon Laughlin, Complt., VS Robert Massey.

In Chancery continued till next Court for report - William Mountague, Complt., VS James & Henry Ritchie, Deft.

In Chancery continued till next Court - Paulin Anderson and others, Comlt. VS William Churchill and others, Deft.

Settlement of William Roane, Admin. of John Murray's Estate continued till next Court.

Page 59

In Chancery continued till next Court - William Churchill, Complt., VS Francis Willis, Esqr., Deft.

In Chancery - Carter Braxton, Complt. VS Richard Corbin & Ralph Wormeley, Esqr., of Christopher Robinson, Esqr., continued till next Court.

Settlement of Berry's Estate continued till next Court.

In Chancery till next Court for Bill - William Jones, Complt., VS George Sanders, Deft.

In Chancery till next Court for report - Gibeon Jones, Complt. VS John Blake, Deft.

In Chancery till next Court - William Churchill, Complt. VS Thomas & George Sanders, Deft.

In Chancery till next Court for report – William Mountague & others, Complt. VS Charles Neilson & others, Deft.

In Chancery - William Clayton, of John Clayton, dec'd, Complt. VS Augustine Smith & others, Deft., continued till next Court.

Attachment abates by Deft. death - John & George Fowlers, Pltf., VS John Adore, Deft.

George & Beverley Daniel, of Robert Daniel, dec'd, Pltf. VS George Bird, of Hannah Price, dec'd, Deft., this day came the parties by their attorneys and thereupon came also a Jury – to wit: came the Pltf. their attorney, and thereupon the Jury to wit: Jonathan Denison, Francis Ross, Harry Beverley Yates, Nicholas Tuggle, Henry Chowning, Thomas Crittenden, Warner Blake, Benjamin Kidd, Henry Batchelder, William George, Wilkerson Barzee, and William Roane, who being elected, tried & sworn the truth to speak upon the Issue joined upon their Oaths doth say that the sd. Deft. did assume upon himself in manner and Form as the Pltf. against him hath declared and they do assess the Pltf. damages by occasion of the non-performance of that assumption to the £32,15 shillings, 6 pence, half penny, beside their costs. Therefore, it is considered that the Pltf. recover against the Deft. his damages afsd. in form afsd. assessed and their costs by them in their behalf expended & the sd. Deft. in mercy , etc.

Page 60

In Case - George & Beverley Daniel, Pltf. VS George Bird, of Hannah Price, dec'd, Deft., this day came the Parties by their attorney' and thereupon came also a Jury, to wit: Jonathan Deneson, Francis Ross, Harry Beverley Yates, Nicholas Tuggle, Henry Chowning, Thomas Crittenden, Warner Blake, Benjamin Kidd, William Roane, Henry Batchelder, William George, and Wilkenson Barzee, who being elected, tried and sworn the Truth to speak upon the issue joined, upon their Oaths do say that the Deft. did assume upon himself in manner and form as the Pltf. against him hath declared, and they do assess the Pltf.. Damages by occasion of the non-performance of that assumption to £11, 7 shillings, 11 pence, half-penny besides the costs. Therefore, it is considered that the Pltf. recover against the sd. Deft. therein Damages in form afsd. assessed, and their Costs by them in this behalf Expended and the sd. Deft in Mercy & etc.

On Petition – George & Beverley Daniel,. of Robert Daniel, dec'd, Admin. of John Aldin, dec'd, Pltf. VS Benjamin Williamson, Deft., this day came the Pltf. by their attorney as the Debt in his proper person and the parties being fully heard and mature deliberation thereupon had, it is considered by the Court that the sd. Pltf. recover against the sd. Deft. ____ pounds _____ shillings and their Costs abt. their defense in this behalf expended.

Philip Grymes, Esqr., his Exec., VS John Robinson in Chancery continued till next Court.

Ordered that the Court be adjourned to the Court in Course.

The Minutes of these proceedings were signed by Edmund Berkeley, Gent.

END OF THE ORDER BOOK

****

Middlesex County, Virginia Land Records
Oct 1785 to 1790

The dates of these documents have a few items dated earlier than 1785 and also have a couple others dated in 1791.

The information found in these documents includes various family relationships, some pre-nuptial agreements, the approximate dates of deaths, the names of hundreds of Slaves and their owners, who bought, sold, gifted, or put them up for collateral for land, and used them to pay off the owner's previous debts. Also the main agricultural crop was tobacco which was used in barter and as payment for salaries of officials and purchase of land. If you are looking for dates of birth, death, etc. for those in the Parish of Christ Church, Middlesex Co., VA, including the vital statistics of the Slaves, search the Register of the Parish, which was published but can also be found on-line at the LDS website.

William Churchill was the Recorder for Middlesex Co., VA, and the clerk consistently spelled his name as "CHURCHHILL" in this book. I have spelled the name as "CHURCHILL".

Pg 1. 24 Oct 1785. Thomas Segar, William Murray and William Churchill are bound to Patrick Henry, Gov. of VA, £1,000. The Condition is the Thomas Segar appointed Sheriff of Middlesex Co, during the pleasure of the sd. Gov. on 11 Aug last past and that he will perform the duties of the office regarding all sums of money and tobacco received by him, etc. Wits.: None. Signed: Thomas Segar, Wm. Murray, Will Churchill. Ackn.: 24 Oct 1785, at the Court House, Urbanna, Middlesex Co., VA.

Pg 1. 24 Oct 1785. Thomas Segar, William Murray and William Churchill are bound to Jaqulen Ambler, Esqr., Treasurer of VA., in the sum of £10,000. The Condition is that Segar shall collect amount for taxes in Middlesex Co. per the act of the Assembly. Wits.: None. Signed: Thomas Segar, Wm. Murray, Will Churchill. Ackn.: 24 Oct 1785, at the Court House, Urbanna, Middlesex Co., VA.

Pg 1. 4 Oct 1785. William Jefferes and Esther, his wife, of Middlesex Co., VA, sell to Philip Lee of the afsd. place, for £130, for a certain tr. of land in Middlesex Co., being 125 a.; bnd. by the land of John Cornelius, Richard Street, John Clark, Senr., Josiah Mc Tyre, Henry Street's heirs, and John Clark, Junr., it being land and plantation wch. sd. Jefferes bot. from Robert Hay, late of Middlesex Co. Wits.: William Jackson, Leonard Jackson, Gawin Jackson, Elizabeth Thurstone made her mark. Signed: Wm. Jeffries, Esther Jeffries,

64

made her mark. Ackn.: 24 Oct 1785, Middlesex Co. Court House, Urbanna –
Will Churchill.

Pg 3. 8 Sep 1785. I, Hugh Walker of Middlesex Co., VA for diverse and good
causes and valuable consideration, do give and grant to Jonathan Denison, of the
afsd. place, **four (4) Negroes – Edy, Tom, Polly & Sam and their Increase.**
Wits.: John T. Walker, Mary Walker. Signed: Hugh Walker. Ackn.: 28 Nov
1785 – This Deed Poll from Hugh Walker to Jonathan Denison was recorded at
Middlesex Co. Court House, Urbanna. – Will Churchill.

Pg 3. 10 Sep 1785. James Mills & Co., merchants, of Middlesex Co., VA, sell
to Simon Laughlin, of the afsd. place, for £21,19 shillings, 6 pence farthing,
wch. the sd. Laughlin is justly indebted to the sd. Mills Co., and for further
consideration of the sum of 5 shillings to sd. Laughlin, do hereby ackn. and
exonerate the Mills Co., etc., he the sd. Laughlin hath granted unto James Mills
& Co. forever – **Peggy and her children, Milly, Lewis, Harry, Sally &
George with all their future Increase,** to have and to hold belonging to the
Premises hereby granted or to be granted Upon Trust that the sd. Mills Co. (after
the 1st day of January 1786) shall sell for the best price that can be gotten after
giving 10 days public notice the sd. Negroe Slaves and Premises and out of the
money arising from sd. sale shall discharge and satisfy the sd. Mills Co. the
£21,19 shillings, 6 pence farthing, with interest from 1 Jan 1776 until the same
shall be fully discharged. Wits.: Geo. Davis, Jas. Ross. Signed: Simon
Laughlin. Ackn.: 23 Jan 1786 – This Deed In Trust was recorded at Middlesex
Co. Court House, Urbanna. – Will Churchill.

Pg 4. 17 Oct 1785. Avy Southern of Middlesex Co., VA, sells to John Good, of
the same Co., for £?, for a certain piece of land in the sd. Co., being 36 a. wch. is
my full part of land left to me by my brother, George Southern. Wits.: James
Lee, George Gardner, Richard Lee. Signed: Avy Southern. Ackn.: 23 Jan 1786
– This Deed In Trust was recorded at Middlesex Co. Court House, Urbanna. –
Will Churchill.

Pg 5. 5 Jan 1786. Thomas Crittenden, of Middlesex Co., VA, sells to George
Saunders, of the afsd. place, for £120, for a certain piece of land in the sd. Co.,
beg. at a point in a branch as a corner to George Saunders and Benjamin
Williamson, down the sd. run of the branch, and then several courses to a point
in Yates' line and the some courses to the main road and then along same and
the to the corner of afsd. Saunders and then several courses to the beg., being
130.75 a. Wits.: Benjamin Williamson, Bartholomew Bristow, Robert
Chowning, Nelson Williamson. Ackn.: 23 Jan 1786 – This Deed was recorded
at Middlesex Co. Court House, Urbanna – Will Churchill.

Pg 6. 27 Mar 1786. William Clemmens, and his wife, Ann, of Gloucester Co., VA, sell to John Healy, of Middlesex Co., VA, for £47, for a piece of land in Middlesex Co. afsd. , beg. at a point at the head of a branch on the south sides [can't read] heirs to a corner [can't read] binding on James Lee to a corner and then several courses to the beg., being 50 a. Wits.: James Lee, Thomas Blake, John Thurston. Signed: William Claments, Ann Claments. Ackn.: 23 Jan 1786 – This Indenture was recorded at Middlesex Co. Court House, Urbanna. – Will Churchill.

Pg. 7. 24 Oct 1785. John Mullins, John Owen, and Anderson Miller are bound unto Patrick Henry, Gov. of VA, in the amount of £500. The Condition is that John Mullins has produced credentials of his Ordination and of his being in regular communion with the Christian Society of Baptists and has obtained a certificate from Middlesex Co. Court empowering him to celebrate Matrimony agreeable to the form established in the sd. Church. Now, if the sd. John Mullins in the performing of this trust, shall conduct himself agreeable to an Act of Assembly passed in the City of Richmond, October Session 1784, Entitled " An Act to regulate the Solemnization of Marriage." Then the above obligation to be void. Signed: John Mullins, John Owen, Anderson Miller. Ackn.: 24 Oct 1785 – This Bond was recorded at Middlesex Co. Court House, Urbanna. – Will Churchill.

Pg 8. 2 Aug 1785. I, John Dean, of Middlesex Co., VA for £150 paid to me by Thomas Healy, of the afsd. place, have hereby sold and do deliver unto the sd. Healy, **three (3) Negroes – that is a man named Isaac, a girl named Fanny and a girl named Lucy.** Wits.: John George, Junr., Nicholas Tuggle. Signed: John Dean. Ackn.: 28 Mar 1786 - This Bill of Sale was recorded at Middlesex Co. Court House, Urbanna. – Will Churchill.

Pg 8. 4 Mar 1786. I, Nelson Daniel, late of Middlesex Co., VA, have appointed by these Presents Col. George Daniel as my lawful Power of Attorney in my place. Wits.: William Segar, Frances Daniel, William Newcomb, made his mark. Signed: N. Daniel. Ackn.: 25 Apr 1786 - This Power of Attorney was recorded at Middlesex Co. Court House, Urbanna. – Will Churchill.

Pg 9. 8 Jun 1786. William Jones, Junr. of Middlesex Co., VA, and Elizabeth, his wife, sell to John Humphries, Sen., of the afsd. place, for £16, for a piece of land in the afsd. Co., being 16 a., beg. at a point in Sandy Branch on the s. side of the run adj. Auguston Smith, dec'd, that was a corner betw. sd. Jones and John Humphries, then joining the sd. Smith's line and then s. down the sd. branch to a corner betw. sd. Jones and Humphries, and then a courses back to the beg. Wit.: None. Signed: Wm. Jones, Elizabeth Jones. Ackn.: 26 Jun 1786 - This Indenture was recorded at Middlesex Co. Court House, Urbanna. – Will Churchill.

Pg 10. I, William Jones, of Middlesex Co., VA, am bound unto John Humphries, of the afsd. place, for £100. The Condition is that he fulfill the obligations of the deed. Wit.: None. Signed: Wm. Jones. Ackn.: 26 Jun 1786 - This Bond was recorded at Middlesex Co. Court House, Urbanna. – Will Churchill.

Pg 11. 25 Jun 1786. Hugh Walker and Catharine, his wife, of Middlesex Co., VA, sell to Littleton Whatson, of the afsd. place, for £270, for a tr. of land in the Parish of Christ Church, being 270 a., beg. at a point and then numerous surveyor's courses down to the count road and then to the beg. Wits.: Peter Montague, Thos. Montague, Maurice Smith, William Morgan. Signed: Hugh Walker, Catharine Walker. Ackn.: 26 Jun 1786 - This Indenture was recorded at Middlesex Co. Court House, Urbanna. – Will Churchill.

Pg 12. 25 Jun 1786. Littleton Whatson, of Middlesex Co., VA., sells to Hugh Walker, of the afsd. place, for £270, for a tr. of land betw. Ralph Wormeley's tr. in sd. Co., adj. Major Smith's as per deed given you, including all appurtenances **including the Negroes as follows and their Increase "Rapper a Fellow, Lucy a Wench, Cate ditto, Ben Fellow, Rachel a Wench & Increase."** However, if the sd. Whatson pay the sale price and expenses from 1 Jan 1786 to this present date of the Deed, then the deed to be void. And, if sd. Whatson fails to pay the sale price with interest, on notice of 10 days the sd. Walker may sell the mortgaged land and Negroes to the highest bidder at public auction. Wits.: Maurice Smith, Peter Montague, William Morgan. Signed: Littleton Watson. Signed: Hugh Walker, Catharine Walker. Ackn.: 26 Jun 1786 - This Mortgage from Watson to Walker was recorded at Middlesex Co. Court House, Urbanna. – Will Churchill.

Pg 13. 28[?] Jul 1786. William Gest and Mary, his wife, of Middlesex Co., VA, sells to George Bird, of the afsd. place, for £24, 10 shillings, for a piece of land, being 7 a. and being part of the Dragon Land, lying betw. the Dragon lands of Hugh Walker. And, sd. Gest agrees to allow sd. Bird and his heirs at all times a good cart path through his plantation down to the sd. Dragon land for carting timber. Wits.: John Healy, James Lee, Meacham George. Signed: William Gest, Mary Gest, made her mark. Ackn.: This Indenture was recorded at Middlesex Co. Court House, Urbanna. – Will Churchill.

Pg 14. 20 Jun 1786. William Hackney, and Sary, his wife, of Middlesex Co., VA., sell to Dudley Vaughan, of the afsd. place, for £50, for 50 a. of land whereon I now live and being in the Parish of Christ Church, Middlesex Co., VA, beg. at John Pritchett's Corner on Pianketunk River and then several courses to the beg. Wits.: George Daniel, John Brooking. Signed: Wm. Hackney, Sarah Hackney. Ackn.: 24 Jul 1786 - This Indenture was recorded at Middlesex Co. Court House, Urbanna. – Will Churchill.

Pg. 15. 24 Jul 1786. Maurice Smith and George Bird are firmly bound to Patrick Henry, Gov. of VA, for £500. The Condition is that whereas Maurice Smith is appointed Coroner of the Middlesex Co., , as of 31 May 1786, and the he truly collect fees and dues put into his hands and pay same to the officers to whom the sd. fees are due and shall execute the duties of his office. Wits.: None. Signed: Maurice Smith, Ge. Bird. Ackn.: 24 Jul 1786 - This Bond was recorded at Middlesex Co. Court House, Urbanna. – Will Churchill.

Pg 15. 22 Jul 1775. Christopher Robinson, of Middlesex Co., VA, is firmly bound to Patrick Henry, Gov. of VA, for £500. The Condition is that whereas Hon. Richard Corbin, Esqr., of King & Queen Co., VA, and Ralph Wormeley, Esqr., of Middlesex Co., VA, in the amount of £5,000. Whereas, the afsd. Corbin and Wormeley are the Exec. of the will of Christopher Robinson, dec'd, have delivered unto the above bound Christopher Robinson, the eldest son and heir at law of the sd. Christopher Robinson, dec'd, all the estate and effects of the sd. dec'd. The Condition is that the sd. Christopher Robinson shall pay all just debts etc. against the absd. Estate of his father that are now remaining unpaid and shall hold harmless the sd. Corbin and Wormeley. Wits.: Samuel Klug, W. Graham. Signed: Chr. Robinson. Ackn.: 23 May 1786 - This Bond was proved by the Oath of James Ross, one of the witnesses[?] and was recorded at Middlesex Co. Court House, Urbanna. – Will Churchill.

Pg 16. 27 Mar 1786. John Daniel, and his wife, Elizabeth, of Middlesex Co., VA, and William Thurston, of the afsd. place, and Susanna, his wife, sell to Thomas Fargason Medearest, of the afsd. place., for £100, for a tr. of land in the Parish of Christ Church, being 50 a., beg. at a point near the Rough Swamp and then several courses to William Thurston's line and the several courses back to the beg. Wits.: W. George, Benjamin Williamson, Samuel Brooks, Thomas Chowning. Signed: John Daniel, William Thurston, made his mark. Ackn.: 25 Sep 1786 - This Indenture was recorded at Middlesex Co. Court House, Urbanna. – Will Churchill.

Pg 17. 25 Sep 1786. William Jones, Senr., Middlesex Co., VA, and Ann, his wife, sell to John Humphris, at the afsd. place, for £12, for a piece of land in the afsd. place, being 15 a., beg. at a pointon the e. side of Meacham's Ferry Road by the fork of the 2 roads close by John Atkinson's orchard fence and then along the sd. road as it stands now up to the fork of the roads next to Thomas Saunders' till it comes in the main road that goes to the Chapple joining the lands of John Atkerson, John Humphris and Thomas Saunders, then a corner in the fork o f the roads from thence abiding by the road that goes to Bushapack [?] as a line betw. sd. Saunders and sd. Humphris till it comes to Blackburn's side line on the n. side of the road then joining Blackburn's line till it comes to the road again and then a course as the road runs a line betw. William Jones and sd.

Humphris, and then several courses to the beg. Wits.: None. Signed: Wm. Jones, Ann Jones, made her mark. Ackn.: 25 Sep 1786 - This Indenture was recorded at Middlesex Co. Court House, Urbanna. – Will Churchill.

Pg 18. 25 Sep 1786. I, William Jones, of Middlesex Co., VA, am firmly bound to John Humphris, of the afsd. place, for £50. The Condition is that William Jones, Senr., perform the articles in the absd. Indenture. Ackn.: 25 Sep 1786 - This Bond was recorded at Middlesex Co. Court House, Urbanna. – Will Churchill.

Pg 19. 20 Sep 1786. William Kidd, and Rachel, his wife, of Middlesex Co., VA, sells to John George, Junr., of the afsd. place, for £60, a piece of land in the afsd. Co., beg. at a point by the swamp side of the White Oak Swamp, being the land of Robert Thurston, dec'd; bnd. by land a straight course of old marhead trees and then to a line of Daniel Dejarnatt and then a course to the road side on Hugh[?] Walker's line, and then several courses to the beg. And, William Kidd and Rachel, his wife freely relinquish all her Right to Dower in the sd. premises. Wits.: Benjamin Williamson, John Thurston, George Blackley, John Kidd. Signed: William Kidd and Rachel Kidd, both made their mark. Ackn.: 25 Sep 1786 - This Indenture was recorded at Middlesex Co. Court House, Urbanna. – Will Churchill.

Pg 20. 23 Oct 1786. Harry Batchelder, and Elizabeth, his wife, of Middlesex Co., VA, sells to Thomas Healy, of the afsd. place., for £33, for a certain piece of land in the sd. Co. bnd. by one-third of 163 a., wch. form. belonged to John Dillard , dec'd, adj. the land of Benjamin Kidd & Henry Washington, dec'd, and the land of the sd. Healy's, wch. was form. Smith's and then a course adj. the land of John Mickelburrough's and land wch. was Sarah Dudley's and then [can't read] George Dillard's, being 50 a. Wits.: John Quarles, Wm. Wood. Signed: Henry Batchelder, Elizabeth Batchelder. Ackn.: 23 Oct 1786 - This Indenture was recorded at Middlesex Co. Court House, Urbanna. – Will Churchill.

Pg 21. 28 Aug 1786. John Jackson and Catharine, his wife, of Middlesex Co., sell to Leonard Jackson, of the afsd, place, for the natural love and affection that he bears to his brother, Leonard, and for the sum of £5, for a certain piece of land in the afsd. Co., being 200 a. , beg. at a point on the branch (can't read) William Jackson [can't read] belonging to William Jackson and then along the swamp, and courses joining the lands of William Jackson, Henry Thurston, and lands of Philip Warwick to the old mill bridge and then up the mill swamp to the beg. place. It being the land and plantation wch. John Jackson (wch. John Jackson since dec'd) Father to John Jackson, who is party to these Presents, bequeathed to his son, Thomas Jackson, by his last will and the sd. Thomas

Jackson departed this life while an infant under the age of 21 years, the sd. land descended to the sd. John Jackson of these Presents, as heir at Law & herein reversion to his sd. brother Thomas Jackson, dec'd. Wits.: Henry Vass, Junr., Warner Blake, Thos. Mountague. Signed: John Jackson. Ackn.: This Indenture of Deed of Gift was recorded at Middlesex Co. Court House, Urbanna. – Will Churchill.

Pg 23. 5 May 1783. 22 Jan 1787 – James Stiff and William Churchill are firmly bound unto Patrick Henry, Gov. of VA, in the sum of £1,000. The Condition is that James Stiff as appointed an additional Inspector of Tobacco at the public warehouse at Kemps[?], Middlesex Co. and that he honestly perform his duties per the Act of the Assembly passed on 5 May 1783. Wits.: None. Signed: Jas. Stiff, Will Churchill. Ackn.: 28 Jan 1787 - This Bond was recorded at Middlesex Co. Court House, Urbanna. – Will Churchill.

Pg 23. 15 Jan 1787. Staige Davis, of Middlesex Co., VA, sells to Thomas Falkner, of the afsd. place, for £25, **for wch. it is for the sole use of and benefit of Andrew Davis, father of the sd. Staige, sells to sd. Thomas Falkner and Evey Falkner, his sister,** during their natural lives, and after their deceases to revert back to Staige Davis and his heirs, being a tr. of land on Piankatonk River in the Parish of Christ Church, wch. is known by the name of Falkner's, being 30 a. Wits.: Jas. Ross, John Segar, Geo. Davis. Ackn.: 26 Feb 1787 - This Indenture was recorded at Middlesex Co. Court House, Urbanna. – Will Churchill.

Pg 24. 1 Jan 1787. Ralph Wormeley, Junr., of Rosegill, Middlesex Co., VA, leases to Robert Spratt, Physician, of Urbanna, Middlesex Co., VA, for 5 shillings, and also for an in consideration of the annual rent of one hoghead of crop tobacco weighing at least 1,000 lbs. net, to be paid by sd. Spratt to the afsd. Wormeley, for a farm letten to sd. Spratt for a term of 10 years, beginning 1 Jan 1787, wch. is the detached plantation on Dragon Swamp, bnd. on the upper end by Jack Murray, and on the lower by those of Robert Murray Inspector, being 150 a. or 152 a. And, that sd. Spratt shall not cut down more of the highland than 50 a. and that adjacent to the land already cleared, except the fresh land wch. he is permitted to tend 3 years and shall annually after the first year of holding the leaves, change the cornfield annually wch. shall at least be [?] unless he dung or mould them, and that he will leave the land under proper term and he (Spratt) reserves to himself the right of getting shingles plank, etc. And, sd. Spratt shall not part with the term except to one of his children, in case of death but to no other person. And, he can sew small grain after his corn crop. Wits.: Overton Cosby, Philip L. Grymes. Signed: Ralph Wormeley, Junr., Robert Spratt. Ackn.: 26 Feb 1787 - This Covenant and Indenture of Lease was recorded at Middlesex Co. Court House, Urbanna. – Will Churchill.

Pg 25. 1 Jan 1787. Charles Edwards, of Middlesex Co. VA, sells to Thomas
Hunton, Junr., of Lancaster Co., VA, for £350, for land in his actual possession,
wch. is in the Parish of Christ Church, Middlesex Co., being 351 a., beg. at a
point on the fork of the Barbeque Creek, and then to a point on the
Rappahannock River side and then down same to the mouth of the Barbeque
Creek and then down the meander to the beg. Wits.: Thomas Hunton, Robert
Ferguson, James Pollard. Signed: Charles Edwards. Ackn.: 26 Feb 1787 - This
Indenture of Lease was recorded at Middlesex Co. Court House, Urbanna. –
Will Churchill.

Pg 26. 26 Feb 1787. John Carter & Martha, his wife, of Lancaster Co., VA,
sells to Thomas Healy, of Middlesex Co., VA, for £40, for a piece of land in
Middlesex Co., beg. at a point on the main county road to a corner betw. the tr.
that sd. Healy bot. of Thomas Smith and the land [can't read] Road to the fork at
[can't read] the main county road to a piece of land Benjamin Kidd bot. of
George Dillard and [can't read] by Thacker Washington's land to the tr. wch.
was form. Smith's, and then to the beg., being one-third of the land mentioned in
the bounds, wch. is 54 a., and one-third. Wits.: W. Segar, James Dunlevy,
Thomas Burk. Signed: John Carter, Martha Carter. Ackn.: 24 Feb 1787 - This
Indenture was recorded at Middlesex Co. Court House, Urbanna. – Will
Churchill.

Pg 27. 26 Mar 1787. Harry Dudley, William Fleet, Baylor Fleet, are firmly
bound to Edmund Randolph, Esqr., Gov. of VA, for £1,000. The Condition is
that Harry Dudley was appointed Searcher for the District of Urbanna, and that
he fulfill the obligations of his office. Wits.: None Signed: Harry Dudley, Wm.
Fleet, Baylor Fleet. Ackn.: 26 Mar 1787 - This Bond was recorded at Middlesex
Co. Court House, Urbanna. – Will Churchill.

Pg 28. 2 Jun 1787. In VA bef. the Court of Middlesex Co., appeared Ralph
Wormeley, Junr., Esqr., of Rosegill, Middlesex Co., VA, , one of the Acting
Executors of the Hon. John Taylor, of Mount Airy, Richmond Co, VA, who
declared to the Court that from the great Trust and Confidence, that he the sd.
appearer reporth in John Randolph Grymes, Esqr., of Brompton Row, London;
NOW KNOW all men that by these Presents that he the sd. Wormeley, Executor
of the sd. Taylor, at the request and by the consent of the other acting Executors
– Francis Lightfoot Lee, Mann Page, and Warner Lewis, Esqrs., whose distant
dwellings from this Co. render their appearance inconvenient, hath made,
ordained, constituted and appointed, by these Presents … in his place and stead
the sd. John Randolph Grymes, his true and lawful Attorney for him the
constituted Executor of the sd. John Taylor, and do hereby empower his sd.
Attorney to ask, claim, demand, etc of and from all person s in Great Britain all
sums of money, etc. owing to the Testator , the Hon. John Taylor by Bond, note,

bill, etc. with all interest now due or that [and it continues on]. Wits.:
Magistrates of Middlesex Co. - Overton Cosby, Edmd. Berkeley, Geoe. Daniel.
Signed: Ralph Wormeley. Ackn.: William Churchill, Clerk of the Court of
Middlesex Co., VA, does attest that the bef. mentioned Power of Attorney was
duly executed, signed and sealed and delivered, for the several uses expressed
therein mentioned by Ralph Wormeley, Junr., one of the Acting Executors of the
Hon. John Taylor, whose name and seal is thereunto affixed, given and granted
in VA, being first witnessed by – Will Churchill. Ackn.: 2 Jun 1787 - This
Power of Attorney from Ralph Wormeley, Junr., one of the Acting Executors of
the Hon. John Taylor, dec'd, to John Randolph Grymes, Esqr., was ackn. by the
sd. Ralph Wormeley to be his Act and Deed and Ordered to be recorded at
Middlesex Co. Court House, Urbanna. – Will Churchill.

Pg 29. 31 Feb 1787 – Joanna Curtis, of Middlesex Co., VA, sell to John Curtis
of the afsd. place, for £50, for 50 a. of land being part of the tr. of land whereon
the sd. Joanna Curtis is now possessed of. Wits.: Peter Kemp, Dudley Bernard.
Chas. Curtis. Signed: Joanna Curtis. Ackn.: 31 Mar 1787 - This Indenture was
recorded at Middlesex Co. Court House, Urbanna. – Will Churchill.

Pg 30. 21 Jun 1775. John Mitchell & Co., of Portsmouth, VA, is firmly bound
unto John Mc Donall[?] & Co., of Glasgow, for £3,389, 3 shillings, 1 penny, to
be paid to the attorney of the sd. Mc Donall & Co. The Condition is that the sd.
Mitchell & Co. pay £1,694,11 shillings, 6 pence on or bef. 14 Nov 1776 with
interest from 14 May 1776. Wits: Robert Burton, Simon Fraser. Signed; Jno.
Mitchell. Ackn.: 30 May 1787 - This Bond was recorded at Middlesex Co.
Court House, Urbanna. – Will Churchill.

Pg 30. 21 Jun 1775. John Mitchell & Co., of Portsmouth, VA, is firmly bound
unto John Mc Donall[?] & Co., of Glasgow, for £3,390 to be paid to the attorney
of the sd. Mc Donall & Co. The Condition is that the sd. Mitchell & Co. pay
£1,695 on or bef. 20 May 1776 with interest from 14 Nov 1775. Wits: Robert
Burton, Simon Fraser. Signed: Jno. Mitchell. Ackn.: 30 May 1787 - This Bond
was recorded at Middlesex Co. Court House, Urbanna. – Will Churchill.

Pg 31. 20 Feb 1787. William Elliott, eldest son and heir at law and acting Exec.
of the last will of Elizabeth Elliott (late of Middlesex Co.), dec'd, and Matthew
Elliott, another son and devisee of the afsd. Elizabeth Elliott, and Overton Cosby
and James Ross, executors of the last will of James Mills, Esqr., of the one part
and Philip Ludwell Grymes, of Brandon, in the afsd. Co., of the other part.
WHEREAS, at a Court in Middlesex Co., on 27 Apr 1784, a suit in Chancery
defending therein betw. the sd. Cosby and Ross as acting Exec. of the last will of
the sd. James Mills, Plaintiff and the sd. William Elliott, as Exec. of the will of
the afsd. Elizabeth, it was decided, the Defendant having stood out all process of
contempt and failing to appear and Answer the Plaintiff's bill on the motion of
the Plaintiff by counsel, there it is decreed that the Defendant to henceforth

barred and foreclosed of [can't read] all equity of redemption in and to the Mortgaged Premises of 550 a. of land and the water grist mill and slaves and personal chattels [can't read] in the deed of mortgage mentioned and referred to in the Plaintiffs' bill, that the Plaintiffs make sale of the land, mill, **slaves**, etc. to the highest bidder for ready money at a 10 day notice of public auction. And, the plaintiffs will apply the money realized are to first discharge the debt due of the mortgage being £255, 14 shillings, 1 penny with lawful interest from 28 Jul, 1772 to the time of sale, next to discharge the debt due to James Mills and Company, being £9, 5 shillings, 2 pence, 1 farthing, with lawful interest from 15 Feb 1775 to the time of payment, and last that the surplus be paid unto the Defendant and that the Defendant to pay unto the Plaintiff their costs. AND, WHEREAS, the sd. Plaintiffs after giving 10 days notice of the sale time and place on 23 Aug 1784 at Urbanna, exposed it for sale and that Philip Ludwell Grymes was the highest bidder at £610. NOW, THIS INDENTURE, that the same William Elliott as eldest son and heir at law and Acting Executor of the will of Elizabeth Elliott and Matthew Elliott and devisee of afsd. Elizabeth, and afsd. Cosby & Ross, as acting Executor of the afsd. James Mills in pursuance of the sd. devisee and also for the sum of £99, 2 shillings, 6 pence to the sd. William Elliott and of the further sum £99, 2 shillings, 6 pence to Matthew Elliott, and £411, 15 shillings to the sd. Overton Cosby and James Ross paid by afsd. Grymes. And, to sd. Grymes is the tr. of land and the water grist mill thereon in the Parish of Christ Church, and to the plat thereof annexes 623 a. described in the survey by the name Mrs. Elizabeth Elliott's part and being the same land wch. was mortgaged as afsd. Wits.: Frances Ross, William Stiff, James Stiff, Thomas Churchill. Signed: Wm. Elliott, Overton Cosby and James Ross, for James Mills, dec'd. Ackn.: 24 Apr 1787 – certified. 28 May 1787 - This Indenture was recorded at Middlesex Co. Court House, Urbanna. – Will Churchill.

Pg 33. 16 Apr 1787. William Churchill, and Elizabeth, his wife, of the Parish of Christ Church, Middlesex Co., VA, sell to Benjamin Churchill, of the afsd. place, for the natural affection and love thy bear unto the sd. Benjamin and also for one ear of Indian corn annually during their natural lives, for a tr. of land in the afsd. place, being 200 a., beg. at a cove where Curril Blade lives, then up the cove and swamp to a point at the head of the swamp and then to Benjamin Hackney's line and then along sd. line to the line of Richard Davis, and then along to Churchill's Mill Creek and then down the Mill Creek to the beg., to have and to hold the land during the term of the natural lives of the sd, William and Elizabeth Churchill. Wits.: Chn. Robinson, Tho. Corbin, Thos. Churchill. Signed: Will Churchill, Eliza Churchill, Benja. Churchill. Ackn.: 23 Apr 1787 – This Indenture was recorded at Middlesex Co. Court House, Urbanna.

Pg 34. 23 Sep 1786. William Churchill, of Middlesex Co., VA., leases to George Standard [Stanard], and Anna, his wife, of King & Queen Co., VA, for one pepper corn during the life of the sd. George and during the widowhood of the sd. Anna, should she survive the death of her husband, and no longer, one certain tr. of land in Middlesex Co., VA, , being 86 a., and known by the name of Humphrie's plantation, and bounded by my hereafter plat. They are not to cut and waste the timber or convert it to any other use but by appropriately to the use of the plantation place. Wits.: Benja. Churchill, James Bradfort, Chr. Robinson. Signed: Will Churchill, Geo. Standard. Ackn.: 23 Apr 1787 –This Indenture was recorded at Middlesex Co. Court House, Urbanna. – Will Churchill.

Pg 35. 23 Apr 1787. William Stiff, of one part, [no location] grants to James Stiff, son of the afsd. William, of the other part, for the affection and love he bears unto the sd. James, a tr. of land lying in the Parish of Christ Church, Middlesex Co., VA, by a plat made by Henry Thackin[?], on 3 Dec 1744, for 284 a., 22 poles, out of my tr. of 736[?] a. Wits.: None. Signed: William Stiff. Ackn.: 23 Apr 1787 –This Indenture was recorded at Middlesex Co. Court House, Urbanna. – Will Churchill.

Pg 35. 3 Apr 1787. Mary Kemp, of Middlesex Co., VA, grants to Cary Kemp, of the afsd. place, for the low and affection she bears towards the afsd. Cary, for a tr. of land that the sd. Mary Kemp is now, or may be possessed of. Wits.: John Curtis, Thomas Kemp, Peter Kemp. Signed: Mary Kemp. Ackn.: 23 Apr 1787 –This Deed was recorded at Middlesex Co. Court House, Urbanna. – Will Churchill.

Pg 36. 23 Sep 1786. John Thilman and Ann, his wife, of Caroline Co., VA, sells to Henry Vass, Junr., of Middlesex Co., VA, for £72, 10 shillings, for a person piece of land in the Parish of Christ Church, Middlesex Co., VA, being 72.5 a., for 100 a., beg. at a point near the house and then to a branch that divides the land & Charles Lee's, and then several courses to John Jackson's and then to a point on the n.w. side of the road in the sd. Jackson's line and then several courses to the beg. Wits.: [?] Rawlins, Junr., Daniel Dejarnatt, Susannah Dejarnatt, Philip Mountague, Henry Vass, Thos. Mountague. Signed: John Thillman, Anne Thillman. Ackn.: 23 Apr 1787 –This Deed was recorded at Middlesex Co. Court House, Urbanna. – Will Churchill.

Pg 38. Commonwealth of Virginia – George Guy, Vivion Minor, and James Sutton … Gent. Whereas, John Thilman and Ann, his wife, of Caroline Co., VA, by their Indenture, dated 23 Sep 1786, sold & conveyed to Henry Vass, Junr., of Middlesex Co., VA, for 100 a. in Middlesex Co. afsd. And, being Anne cannot travel, G. Guy and V. Minor privately examined her on 19 Oct 1786. Ackn.: 23 Apr 1787 –This Indenture was recorded at Middlesex Co. Court House, Urbanna. – Will Churchill.

Pg 39. 27 Feb 1780. Simon Laughlin of Middlesex Co., VA, and Ann, his wife, sell to James Wortham, of the afsd. place, for £25, for a tr. of land and plantation in the afsd. place, and wch. tr. of delivered to the sd. Laughlin by Thomas Laughlin, dec'd, by his will, who bot. the land from John Moseley, Elizabeth Moseley, James George, and Agathy George, and binding on the land of Ralph Wormeley, Sen., the land of John Wortham, and on the land of Benjamin [can't read] and Robert Murray and the land of Ambrose Canady, dec'd, being 75 a. Wits.: Charles Collier[?], James Wortham, Thomas Roan. Signed; Simon Laughlin, Ann Laughlin. 6 Jan 1785 – William Churchill examined Ann Laughlin. Ackn.: 24 Apr 1787 - This Indenture was recorded at Middlesex Co. Court House, Urbanna. – Will Churchill.

Pg 40. 5 Jan 1781[?]. Robert Daniel, James Lee, and Robert Daniel, Junr., of Middlesex Co., VA, are firmly bound unto James Gregorie and George Lorimer, Exec. of the will of John Daniel, late of the town of Urbanna, Middlesex Co., VA, dec'd., in the sum of £50,000[?]. The Condition is that Robert Daniel and James Lee, Guardians and Trustees to the Orphans of the sd. John Daniel, dec'd, request a division of the sd. Estate obtained by an Order of the Court for the same, but the sd. Estate not being settled, the sd. Robert Daniel and James Lee, and Robert Daniel, Junr. for themselves and their heirs do herby agree to indemnify the sd. James Gregorie and George Lorimer from all debts and demand, wch. are now due or may have been from the Estate of John Daniel, dec'd. Wits.: Thomas Segar, Benjamin Kidd. Signed: Robert Daniel, James Lee, Robert Daniel, Junr. Ackn.: 28 May 1787 – This Bond was recorded at Middlesex Co. Court House, Urbanna. – Will Churchill.

Pg 41. 24 Feb 1787. John George, Junr., of Middlesex Co., VA, sells to Benjamin Seward[?], of the afsd. place, after being paid [no amount], sells to the Seward[?]a piece of land in the afsd. Co., beg. at a point on the side of White Oak Swamp cornering on the land lots the property of Carter Thurston, bnd. by a line n.w. to a corner of sd. Thurston and Daniel Dejarnett and then to a corner of Hugh Walker and then several courses to the beg., being 50 a. Wits.: George Pasquet, Staige Davis, George Davis. Signed: John George, Junr., Susanna George. Ackn.: 25 June 1787 – This Indenture was recorded at Middlesex Co. Court House, Urbanna. – Will Churchill.

Pg 42. ___ June 1787. Whereas, Thomas Kemp, late of Middlesex Co., dec'd, did in his lifetime obtain a grant for 400 a., of land in Louisa Co., VA, but since by a division of the sd. Co., is now situated in Albemarle Co., VA, and the sd. grant will appear of Record in the General Court, in the following VA set: At a

Court held at the Capitol on 21 Apr 1772, Thomas Kemp having petitioned the late President of his Majesty's Council for a grant of 400 a. of land in Louisa granted by Patent, 22 Nov 1752 to Christopher Curtis lapsed for non-payment of the quit rents from Christopher Robinson, Esqr., Robert Daniel and George Daniel, Esqrs., of the sd. Christopher Curtis, dec'd. Christopher Curtis, son and heir of the afsd. Christopher Curtis, his came the Petition by his attorney and the

Defts. Christopher Robinson and Robert Daniel being dead, and the other Defts. having duly summoned the sd. surviving Defts., were solemnly called but came not, therefore it is adjudged by the Court that the sd. forfeited and vested again in the Crown, wch. is certified to the Gov.& that the sd. Thomas Kemp is first Petitioner for the same and hath pursued his Petition with effort. I, Gary Kemp, of Middlesex Co., son and heir of the sd. Thomas Kemp, do by these Presents constitute and appoint in my place and stead, William Curtis, of the afsd. Co., and my lawful Attorney for the purpose of selling for me the sd. grant of land and the sd. Curtis is hereby with full power to sell and dispose of the land, my Right and Title and prepare a deed. Wits.: Chas. Curtis, Chichester Curtis. Signed: Cary Kemp. Ackn.: 25 June 1787 – This Power of Attorney was recorded at Middlesex Co. Court House, Urbanna. – Will Churchill.

Pg 43. 25 Jun 1787. Whereas, Christopher Curtis, of Middlesex Co., VA, by his will, dated 26[?] Dec 1763, directed his Exec. to sell his land in Louisa Co., VA, and is now by a division of sd. Co., in Albemarle Co., VA. I, George Daniel, of Middlesex Co., VA, Exec. of Chichester Curtis, dec'd, do by these Presents appoint in my stead William Curtis of the sd. Middlesex Co., VA, my lawful Power of Attorney in the sole purpose of selling and discharging of the sd. land in now vested and to sell the land, his Right and Title to the lands and to execute a good deed. Wits.: None. Signed: Geo. Daniel. Ackn.: 25 June 1787 – This Power of Attorney was recorded at Middlesex Co. Court House, Urbanna. – Will Churchill.

Pg 43. 8 Jun 1787. I, Thomas Iverson, of Middlesex Co., VA, for diverse good causes and valuable considerations, to grant and confirm unto Philip Lewis, Samuel Morgan Lewis, and William Steptoe Lewis, or in case of death of any one all, then unto the three eldest sons or daughters of Jonathan and Sarah Gayle Lewis, provided the three first mentioned or any of them die bef. they arrive at the age of 21 years or without lawful issue, **a certain Negro girl named Kitty[?], abt. 12 or 14 years of age and her Increase, in Trust** to Sarah Gayle Lewis till the arrive at the above described, to have and to hold and singular the Negro girl named Kitty[?] and her Increase, of me the sd. Thomas Iverson, unto the sd. Phillip Lewis, Sarah Lewis, Samuel Morgan Lewis and William Steptoe Lewis or the three eldest sons or daughters of the sd. Jonathan and Sarah Gayle Lewis or any of the three mentioned, dying under age or without lawful issue, their heirs, Exec., etc, hereforth **to their proper use and uses thereof, and therewith to do, order and dispose, at their wills and pleasure, as of their own proper goods and effects, etc. without any trouble or denial from me.** Wits.: Gary Kemp, Peter Montague. Signed: Thomas Iverson. Ackn.: 25 June 1787 – This Deed Poll was recorded at Middlesex Co. Court House, Urbanna. – Will Churchill.

Pg 44. 8 Jun 1787. I, Thomas Iverson, of Middlesex Co., VA, for diverse good causes and valuable considerations, have given unto the son or dau. of beloved

Aunt Catharine Walker, or nay of her own children, obtaining, a Deed of Gift or other Instrument of writing, under the hand and seal of sd. Catharine Walker, implying the particular son or dau., she [can't read] wish to have the Negro & etc. hereafter described, **a certain Negro girl named Dinah, abt. 10 years of age, and her Increase, in Trust** to have and to hold, of me the sd. Thomas Iverson, unto the sd. particular son or dau. of the sd. Walker, on his or her obtaining a Deed of Gift or otherwise as above described, from the sd. Catharine his or her Execs. etc. from hereafter **to their proper use and uses thereof, and therewith to do, order and dispose, at their wills and pleasure, as of their own proper goods and effects, etc. without any trouble or denial from me.** Wits.: Gary Kemp, Peter Montague. Signed: Thomas Iverson. Ackn.: 25 June 1787 – This Deed Poll was recorded at Middlesex Co. Court House, Urbanna. – Will Churchill.

Pg 45. 24 Mar 1786. William Bowden, and Sally, his wife, of Middlesex Co., VA, sell to Thomas Crittenden, of the afsd. place, for £263, 15 shillings, for a tr. of land in the afsd. Co., being 78 a., butting th elands of John Taylor Corbin, Esqr., Henry Vass, John Segar, Capt. Thomas Segar, it being the land and plantation form. of Henry Shepard late of sd. Co., all except 6.25 a. bot. off of Capt. Segar's land, and of the sd. Segar, William Bowden, and also the sd. William and Sally Bowden. Also, another parcel of land in the afsd. place, being 47.5 a. and bnd. by land of Henry Vass, James Crossfield, Elizabeth Kemp, and William Owens, and wch. land was form. sold to Thomas Crittenden by the afsd. William Owen, and of wch. 6.25 a. was form. conveyed by deed to William Bowden by Thomas Crittenden. Wits.: Thomas Segar, John Jackson, Oliver Yarrington. Signed: William Bowden, Sally Bowden. 26 Jun 1786 – Henry Vass & Philip Mountague examined Sally Bowden. Ackn.: 23 Jul 1787– This Indenture was recorded at Middlesex Co. Court House, Urbanna. – Will Churchill.

Pg 47. 26 May 1787 – George Dame and Mary, his wife, of Middlesex Co., VA., sell to Thomas Crittenden, of the afsd. place, for £33, for a parcel of land in the afsd. place, beg. at a point on the side of the main road and then several courses to a corner of John Corbin, and then to the main road and then back to the beg. on the remainder part of George Dame's land, being 57 a. Wits.: James Lee, James Crossfield, Overton Daniel. Signed: George Dame, Mary Dame, made her mark. Ackn.: 23 Jul 1787– This Indenture was recorded at Middlesex Co. Court House, Urbanna. – Will Churchill.

Pg 48. 5 Mar 1787. Churchill Blakey, of the Parish of Christ Church, Middlesex Co., VA, and Ann, his wife, sell to John Daniel, of the afsd. place, for £300, for a tr. of land in the afsd. place, being 300 a.[?], beg. at a point of the e. side of the main road and a corner to Joan Jafey [Jeffries?] and then along that line to Thomas Brooks' line and then several courses to the mouth of a swamp on William Hardee's line and then to a point in John T. Corbin's[?] line and then along sd. Corbin's line to a corner of Frances Cloudas' line and then along same to and point on the e. side of the main road and then down same to George Dame's line and then along his line to the beg., being 200 a.[?]. Wit.: Charles Daniel , Thomas Brooks, Samuel Jesse, made his mark, [Cenejin?] Carter, William Calaham,[?] made his mark. Signed: Churchill Blakey, Ann Blakey. Ackn.: 23 Jul 1787– This Indenture was recorded at Middlesex Co. Court House, Urbanna. – Will Churchill.

Pg 50. 5 Mar 1787. John Daniel, and Elizabeth, his wife, of the Parish of Christ Church, Middlesex Co., VA, sell to Churchill Blakey, of the afsd. place, for £300, for a tr. of land in the afsd. place, being 299 a., beg. at a point in Hannah Lorimer's line and corner to James Kidd, then to the head of [can't read] and several courses to William Thurston's line and then along same to a branch and then down same to John George's mill pond and then up the saw mill pond and the several courses to Hannah Lorimer's line and then along same to the beg. Wits.: Chester Daniel, Susannah Jessey, made her mark, Thomas Brooks, Cinyon Carter, William Calaham. Signed: John Daniel, Elizabeth Daniel. Ackn.: 23 Jul 1787– This Indenture was recorded at Middlesex Co. Court House, Urbanna. – Will Churchill.

Pg 51. 23 Jul 1787. Henry Vass, Junr., and Elizabeth, his wife, of Middlesex Co., VA, sell to George Dame, of the afsd. place, for £75, 12 shillings, 6 pence, for a piece of land in the afsd. place, beg. at a point and then to a point in the line of John Jackson's heirs and then to a point in the line of William Jones and then along his line to the beg., being 75.5 a. Wits.: None. Signed: Henry Vass, Junr., Elizabeth Vass. Ackn.: 23 Jul 1787– This Indenture was recorded at Middlesex Co. Court House, Urbanna. – Will Churchill.

Pg 52. 23 Jul 1787. Churchill Blakey and Ann, his wife, of Middlesex Co., VA, sells to Thomas Crittenden, of the afsd. place, for £3, 13 shillings, 4 pence, for a piece of land being 3 and two-thirds, beg. at a corner bet. Jas.[?] Daniel and Jane Jesse, and then along a line to the main road, adj. land that was form. taken off the land of Jno. Daniel form. the land of the afsd. Blakey and adj. the land sold and conveyed to Robert Mc Tyre by Col. George Bird, and the sd. Churchill Blakey does relinquish all Right to the sd. land. Wits.: None. Signed: Churchill Blakey, Ann Blakey. Ackn.: 23 Jul 1787– This Indenture was recorded at Middlesex Co. Court House, Urbanna. – Will Churchill.

Pg 53. 30 Apr 1787. Hugh Walker, of Middlesex Co., VA, for good and diverse causes and valuable consideration **do confirm unto my son, Hugh Walker Junr., of the afsd. place, a certain Negro boy, named Nelson, abt. 17 years of age, with all of his profits from this date forward, and who is to be hired annually by Overton Crosby, Esqr. for the best price that can be obtained for bond and security and the money collected and kept in possession of sd. Crosby in Trust till Hugh Walker, Junior arrives at the**

78

age of 21 years. Wits.: Jonathan Denison, George Walker. Signed: Hugh Walker. Ackn.: 25 Jun 1787– This Deed Poll was recorded at Middlesex Co. Court House, Urbanna. – Will Churchill.

Pg 53. 20 Oct. 1787. Peggy Thurston, of Middlesex Co., VA, sells to Thomas Crittenden of the afsd. place, for £500, for a parcel of land lying in the afsd. place, and known by the name of Jones, bnd. upon Richard Corbin, Esqr., and being 400 a. Wits.: W. Segar, James Lee, Carter Thurston. Signed: Peggy Thurston. Ackn.: 25 Feb 1788– This Indenture was recorded at Middlesex Co. Court House, Urbanna. – Will Churchill.

Pg 54. 24 Sep 1787. Robert Dudley, of Middlesex Co., VA, sells to Sarah Bayton and Beverly Bayton, of the afsd. place, for £15, for a parcel of land and plantation in the afsd. place, being 15 a., beg. at a corner in Pritchard's line and then to Morgan's and Pritchard's corner near the road, then several courses to Miller's line and then to Pritchard's corner, and being to the use to the afsd. Sarah during the term of her natural life, with the remainder after her death to the sd. Beverly Bayton and his heirs. Wits.: Dudley Vaughan, Wm. Shackelford, John Craine. Signed: Robert Dudley, made his mark. Ackn.: 24 Sep 1787– This Indenture was recorded at Middlesex Co. Court House, Urbanna. – Will Churchill.

Pg 55. 16 Dec 1786. Susanna Daniel, of Middlesex Co., VA, leases to Lunsford Daniel, of Orange Co., NC, for the consideration of the maintenance during her natural life or widowhood, and on no other amount whatsoever has been given, during the absd. term and no longer all my Right of Dower to **my deceased husband, William Daniel's Estate,** consisting of lands, houses, orchards, water courses, Negro slaves stocks of horses, cattle and sheep, etc. now in possession of the afsd. Susanna Daniel. And, the sd. Lundsford Daniel for his part in bound to furnish to the sd. Susanna Daniel with her now present family with sufficient diet, lodgings and clothing without disposing of any of the real estate for a longer term mentioned and to use the profits from the estate in compliance with the terms. Wits.: John Jackson, John Seward, Mary Daniel. Signed: Susanna Daniel. 2_ Jul 1787 – The Deed of Leases was certified. Ackn.: 24 Sep 1787– This Deed of Lease was recorded at Middlesex Co. Court House, Urbanna. – Will Churchill.

Pg 56. 21 Jun 1787. William Shackelford and Catherine, his wife, of Essex Co, VA, sell to Lunsford Daniel, of Middlesex Co, VA, for £100, for £100, for a parcel of land in the afsd. place, being 273 a., **it being whereon Susanna Daniel, relict of William Daniel, dec'd, late of the afsd. Co. now lives, and part of the land being claimed by the sd. Shackelford by virtue of intermarriage with Catherine Shackelford, his wife, she being one of the co-heiresses of the afsd. William Daniel, dec'd,** and is bnd. by the lands of Thomas Segar, Nelson Daniel, John Jackson, Benjamin Seward, Meacham

George, and Carter Thurston. Wits.: John Seward, Henry D. Shepherd. Signed:
Wm. Shackelford, Catherine, Shackelford. Ackn.: 23 Jul 1787– This Deed was
recorded at Middlesex Co. Court House, Urbanna. – Will Churchill. On 24 Sep
1787, the sd. Catherine relinquished her Right and title to the sd. land and
premises.

Pg 57. 25 Aug 1787. William Churchill and Elizabeth, his wife, and George
Standard and Anna, his wife, of Middlesex Co., VA, sell to Thomas Hanon[?],
[no location], for £43, for a tr. of land in the Parish of Christ Church, the afsd.
Co. , being 43 a. and 69 poles, beg. at the spring running down the creek and
then up Sturgeon Creek and then several courses to the beg. Wits.: None.
Signed: Will Churchill, Eliza Churchill, Geo. Standard. Ackn.: 24 Sep 1787–
This Deed was recorded at Middlesex Co. Court House, Urbanna. – Will
Churchill. On 19 Oct 1789, Elizabeth Churchill and Anna Standard were
examined privately. On 22 Oct 1789, Edmd. Berkeley, Geo. Daniel indicated
they examined the two spouses and on 26 Oct 1789, it was ordered to be
recorded.

Pg 59. 22 Aug 1787. Charles Dudley and Nancy, his wife, of the Parish of
Christ Church, Middlesex Co, VA, sells to John Wake, of the afsd. place, for
£40, 10 shillings, for 40.5 a. in the afsd. place, bnd. by a plat map surveyed by
Robert Billops, the property of Charles Dudley but now sold to John Wake,
lying on the Rappahanock River, beg. at a point in John Wake's line s. side of
Wake's field and then several courses to the e. side of a marsh, and then several
courses to the beg. The land is in the possession of the sd. Wake by an
Indenture of Bargain and Sale to him, made for one year, dated the day bef. the
present document., by turning uses into possessions. Wits.: Ann Wake, John
Wake, Geo. Standard, Frns. Jones, made their mark. Signed: Charles Dudley,
Nancy Dudley. Ackn.: 24 Sep 1787– This Deed was recorded at Middlesex Co.
Court House, Urbanna. – Will Churchill.

Pg 60. 21 Jul 1787. William Hudgin Brummill, of Middlesex Co., VA, sells to
John Layton, of the afsd. place, for £15, for a piece of land in the afsd. place,
being 12 a., beg. at a point on the Gum Branch line wch. the sd. Brummell and
Layton agreed to be a corner betw. each other and then to a line of afsd.
Brummell and Churchill until it meets and point and then to the head of the
branch by Daniel Jefferson's and then down same to another corner and then to
the beg. Wits.: George West, Daniel Jefferson, Philamon Yarrington, made his
mark. Signed: Wm. Hudgin Brummell. Ackn.: 24 Sep 1787– This Deed was
recorded at Middlesex Co. Court House, Urbanna. – Will Churchill.

Pg 62. 21 Jun 1788. Lawrence Meacham, of the Parish of Christ Church,
Middlesex Co., VA, sells to Charles Curtis and John George, Junr., of the afsd.
place, for £70, for "my lotts and houses" in Urbanna and bnd. by lots of Overton
Cosby & 60 & Robert Spratt, Esqr., Upon Trust, that the sd. Curtis and George

80

shall (after 1 Jan 1789, or as soon as either party requests) shall sell them for the best price after 10 days notice at Public Auction, and out of the money arising from the sale satisfy to Charles Curtis and John George, Junr., the above price of £70 with interest from 1 Aug 1787 until it is fully discharged. Wits.: John George, W. George. Signed: L. Meacham. Ackn.: 28 Jul 1788– This Deed was certified and was recorded on 26 Jan 1789, at Middlesex Co. Court House, Urbanna. – Will Churchill.

Pg 63. Thomas Edgar, of the present of Sail[?] Catherine, Middlesex Co., VA, ship carpenter, appoint my loving wife, Anna Maria Edgar, my true and lawful attorney for me in my name to do whatever is necessary whomever it may concern in America or elsewhere re: all sums of money, good, chattels, wares. etc. and whatever is necessary regarding any premises, etc. Wits.: Major Wright, Richd. Willey. Signed: Thomas Edgar. London – Major Wright of Torrington Street in the Parish of Saint George, Middlesex Co, Gent., ackn. witnessing the item with Richard Willey 9 Jul 1788 at the Mansion House, bef. John Burnell, Mayor. Also, John Evans notarized the signature of Major Wright on the afsd. date. Ackn.: Middlesex Co., VA – 29 Oct 1788, the Power of Attorney of Thomas Edgar with the handwriting and seal of Thomas Edgar to his wife, Anna, was recorded.

Pg 65. 29 Oct 1787. William Churchill, of the one part , sells to Thomas Churchill, son of the afsd. William Churchill, of the other part, for the natural love and affection he bears unto the afsd. Thomas, for a tract of land bot. by Armistead Churchill, Esqr., late of Middlesex Co, & William Hill, of the afsd. place, being 100 a. Wits.: None. Signed: Will Churchill. Ackn.: 22 Oct 1787– This Deed was recorded at Middlesex Co. Court House, Urbanna. – Will Churchill.

Pg 65. 27 Oct 1787. William Churchill, of the one part, [no location] leases to George Standard and Anna, his wife, [no location], for one ear of Indian corn yearly, during Standard's life and during the widowhood, of the sd. Anna Standard, should she survive the death of the sd. Standard and no longer, for a certain parcel of land in Middlesex Co., VA., being 80 a.; beg. at a point betw. the land sold by William Churchill to George Blake, Junr., down to sd. Churchill's Mill just n. of the house that George West now live in and up the sd. Mill swamp to John Robinson's line and then along same to the main road and then along it to the beg. Wits.: None. Signed: William Churchill, Geo. Standard. Ackn.: 22 Oct 1787– This Deed was recorded at Middlesex Co. Court House, Urbanna. – Will Churchill.

Pg 66. 22 Oct 1787. Ann Sutton, widow of Rowland Sutton, sells to John Sutton, son of the sd. Ann and Rowland Sutton, dec'd, for the natural love and affection she bears to her son John, and also for better maintenance of him, being all the messuage or tr. of land being 92 a., bot. by her late husband from

Charles Dudley in 1772, being in the part of Middlesex Co, commonly called Pine Top. Wits.: Anderson Miller, Thomas Bush, Sarah Major. Signed: Ann Sutton. Ackn.: 22 Oct 1787– This Deed of Gift was recorded at Middlesex Co. Court House, Urbanna. – Will Churchill.

Pg 67. 17 Feb 1787. Received of Edward Ware my Gardin [Guardian?], £15 that my grandfather, Edward Ware left me in his will to be paid by his Exec. when I come of age of one and twenty years. Wits.: Robt. Ware. Signed Philip Warwick. 31 Aug 1787. Received of Edward Ware £11, 18 shillings, 7 pence, it being the balance of portion of my father's Estate due me from Edward Ware my Gardin [Guardian?]. Philip Warwick. 22 Oct 1787– The absd. receipts were produced in Court and Ordered recorded at Middlesex Co. Court House, Urbanna. – Will Churchill.

Pg 68. 22 Oct 1787[8?]. A deed from William Churchill and Philip Ludwell Grymes as Trustees for the Sale of William Armistead's lands to Andrew Davis was this day produced in open Court by the sd. Davis, who ackn. all his Right and Title to the within mentioned land, contained in the sd. Deed to Staige Davis, wch. is order recorded – Will Churchill.

Pg 68. 30 Jul 1787. John Jackson, planter, of the Parish of Christ Church, Middlesex Co., VA, sells to William Hill, of the afsd. place. WHEREAS, the sd. William Hill is justly indebted to the sd. John Jackson on the sum of £120 in gold and silver at the weight according to law in consideration thereof, the sd. Hill sold & delivered and by these Presents does sell & deliver to the sd. Jackson, the tr. of land in the Low End of the afsd. place, being 150 a., being part of the tract he now lives on, provided always on the Condition never the less that if the sd. William Hill shall pay £120 in gold and silver, on or bef. 27 Feb 1788, then this Indenture will be void. Wits.: Dudley Vaughan, Thomas Boss, John Minter. Signed: William Hill. Ackn.: 26 Feb 1788– This Deed of Mortgage was recorded at Middlesex Co. Court House, Urbanna. – Will Churchill.

Pg 69. 14 Nov 1787. Thomas Crittenden, and Jenny, his wife, of Middlesex Co., VA, sell to Richard Corbin, Esqr., of King & Queen Co., VA, for £400, for 347 a. of land in the Parish of Christ Church, Middlesex Co., VA, bnd. by a Survey done by John Lewis and Robert Beverley in company with a Jury empanelled and sworn on 1 Dec 1770, by an Order of the General Court to settle the bounds of Burnhams, Weekes, and Parrotts Patents now belonging to and in the possession of the sd. Corbin, and also Welch's Patent under wch. the late Lodowick Jones claimed, by whose death is descended in course of descent to his sister Peggy Thurston, as heiress at law and by her conveyed to Thomas Crittenden. Wits.: John Taylor Corbin, Thos. Corbin, Edward Ware. Signed: Thos. Crittenden, Jenny Crittenden. Ackn.: 25 Feb 1788– This Deed was recorded at Middlesex Co. Court House, Urbanna. – Will Churchill.

Pg 70. 24 Nov 1787. Lucy Jones, widow of the late Lodowick Jones, of Middlesex Co., VA, sells to Richard Corbin, of King and Queen Co., VA. WHEREAS, Lucy Jones, relict of Lodowick Jones, dec'd, by virtue of her Dower, is seized of a certain parcel of land whereon her late husband lived, in the afsd. Co. The reversion whereof was in Peggy Thurston. sister of the afsd. Lodowick Jones, and by her conveyed to Thomas Crittenden, and then by Crittenden it was conveyed to Richard Corbin by deed, dated 14 Dec 1787. Now, in consideration of £100 paid to sd. Lucy Jones hereby ackns. and forever acquit and exonerate the afsd. Corbin and does confirm to him all of her interest and claim into the afsd. Dower lands. Wits.: Thos. Healy, Edward Ware, Tho. Corbin. Signed: Lucy Jones. Ackn.: 25 Feb 1788– This Deed was recorded at Middlesex Co. Court House, Urbanna. – Will Churchill.

Pg 71. 2 Jul 1787. William Owen and Jane, his wife, of Middlesex Co., VA, sell to Thom[?] Jackson, of the afsd. place, for £41, 10 shillings, for a parcel of land in the afsd. place, being 41.5 a. , beg. at a point betw. Thomas Crittenden and sd. Jackson, and then along a line to a corner of Crittenden and Betty Kemp and then several courses back to the beg. Wits.: Thomas Segar, W. Segar, Thomas Segar, Junr., Garvin Jackson. Signed; Wm. Owen, Jane Owen. 22 Jan 1788 – Henry Vass and Thomas Segar examined Jane Owen. Ackn.: 25 Feb 1788– This Deed was recorded at Middlesex Co. Court House, Urbanna. – Will Churchill.

Pg 73. 2_ Oct 1787. Nichols Tuggle, and Susanna, his wife, of Middlesex Co., VA, sell to Thomas Healy, of the afsd. place, for £115, 10 shillings, for a certain tr. of land in the Parish of Christ Church, Middlesex Co., being 77 a., beg. at a point near Grange Creek a corner to William Steptoe and then down his line to a point in Washington's line and then numerous courses and then down the creek to the beg. Wits.: W. Segar, W. George, Thomas Segar, S. Meacham. Signed: Nichols Tuggle, Susanna Tuggle, made her mark. Ackn.: 25 Feb 1788– This Deed was recorded at Middlesex Co. Court House, Urbanna. – Will Churchill.

Pg 74. 2 Jun 1787. Robert Murray, Robert Stamper, Thomas Roane, Churchill Blakey are bound to Edmund Randolph, Esqr., Gov. VA, in the amount of £1,000. The Condition is that the above named persons shall collect and pay a certain tax of 6 shillings per hogshead on Tobacco per an Act of the Assembly passed in Oct 1786 in order to have a supply of money in the US Congress assembled. Wits.: None. Signed: Robert Murray, Robert Stamper, Thomas Roane, Churchill Blakey. Ackn.: 2 Jun 1787– This Bond was recorded at Middlesex Co. Court House, Urbanna. – Will Churchill.

Pg 74. 22 Oct 1787. William Stiff, Francis Ross, Edmund Berkeley are firmly bound unto Edmund Randolph, Esqr., Gov. VA, in the amount of £1,000. The Condition is that the above named persons shall collect and pay a certain tax of

6 shillings per hogshead on Tobacco per an Act of the Assembly passed in Oct
1786 in order to have a supply of money in the US Congress assembled. Wits.:
None. Signed: William Stiff, Francis Ross, Edmund Berkeley. Ackn.: 22 Oct
1787– This Bond was recorded at Middlesex Co. Court House, Urbanna. – Will
Churchill.

Pg 75. 22 Oct 1787. John George, Maurice Smith, William Churchill are firmly
bound unto Edmund Randolph, Esqr., Gov. VA, in the amount of £1,000. The
Condition is that John George was appointed Sheriff on 6 Oct and that he well
and truly perform the duties of his office. Wits.: None. Signed: John George,
Maurice Smith, William Churchill. Ackn.: 22 Oct 1787– This Bond was
recorded at Middlesex Co. Court House, Urbanna. – Will Churchill.

Pg 75. 22 Oct 1787. John George, Maurice Smith, William Churchill are firmly
bound unto Jaquilen Ambler, Esqr., Treasurer of VA, in the amount of £10,000.
The Condition is that John George shall collect and account for all taxes
imposed and perform the duties of his office. Wits.: None. Signed: John
George, Maurice Smith, William Churchill. Ackn.: 22 Oct 1787– This Bond
was recorded at Middlesex Co. Court House, Urbanna. – Will Churchill.

Pg 76. 21 Jan 1788. Ann Martin, of Middlesex Co., VA, for the love and good
will she has toward her son, Joseph Martin, of the afsd. place, freely grants unto
him all of her estate, real and personal, of wch. she is seized and possessed, viz.
one cow, 2 head of hogs, 2 beds and furniture 4 chests, 2 tables, 19 plates 2
dishes, 2 pewter basins, 4 earthen plates, 12 cups and saucers 4 flag bottom
chairs, 2 iron pots, one box iron and heaters, 1 skillet, 1 bed and bedstead and
furniture, one dish, knife, and fork . Wits.: Wm. Elliott, Francis Woodley[?],
made his mark, Wm. Jones, Senr., Phileman Yarrington, made his mark,
Thomas Woodley, made his mark. Signed: Ann Martin, made her mark. Ackn.:
25 Feb 1788– This Deed of Gift was recorded at Middlesex Co. Court House,
Urbanna. – Will Churchill.

Pg 76. 5 Sep 1787. James Gregorie, late of Urbanna, Middlesex Co., VA, but
now of Charles Town, SC, the lawful attorney of George Johnson, late of
Gloucester Co., has made and ordained by these Presents by the Power and
Authority to me in behalf given by the sd. Johnson by a Power of Attorney
under his hand dated 25 Jun 1771, does appoint Overton Cosby, of Middlesex
Co., VA to be the attorney of the sd. George Johnson, to do whatever is
necessary to handle his affairs in recovering debts, etc. Wits.: Staige Davis, Geo.
B. Davis. Signed: Ja. Gregorie. Ackn.: 25 Feb 1788– This Power of Attorney
was recorded at Middlesex Co. Court House, Urbanna. – Will Churchill.

Pg 77. 4 Sep 1787. James Gregorie, late of Urbanna, Middlesex Co., VA, but
now of Charles Town, SC, the sole Acting Exec. of the will of David Ker, Esqr.,
late of the afsd. Co., dec'd, have authorized and appointed Overton Cosby and

James Ross, of the afsd. Co., my true and joint attorneys for me in may name to do whatever is necessary regarding the estate of the sd. David Ker Estate. And, they are to have the power to substitute one or more attornies under them with limited power. Wit.: Staige Davis, Geo. B. Davis. Signed: Ja. Gregorie. Ackn.: 25 Feb 1788– This Power of Attorney was recorded at Middlesex Co. Court House, Urbanna. – Will Churchill.

Pg 78. 26 Jul 1787. Winefred G. Montague, [no location] Guardian of Thomas Tarply Montague, orphan of James Montague, dec'd, leases to George Bird, of Middlesex Co., VA, for £10, a lot and farm Letten by these Presents and assigns a certain piece of land, being 40 a., in the afsd. place, beg. at the River and running up a swamp known by the name of Muddy Swamp, including the sd. marsh, then up a Wattow leading to the fork road to William Wood's line, and then along same to a corner and then along a line dividing the land from George Bird's land down to the River, during the time of 9 years and until the full end of the term of the sd. 9 years, or until the absd. Orphan shall arrive at 21 years. Wits.: T. Tarpley, Henry Vass, Junr., William Montague, Thomas Montague. Signed: Winefred G. Montague. 26 Feb 1788– This Deed of Lease was recorded at Middlesex Co. Court House, Urbanna. – Will Churchill.

Pg 79. 28 Feb 1788. Thacker Washington, of King George Co., VA, sells to Charlotte Neilson, Jane Neilson, Agnes Neilson and Mary Elizabeth Mills Neilson, of Middlesex Co., VA, in consideration of the Release of the afsd. Charlotte Neilson of all her Right, Title and Interest in all the real and personal Estate of Henry Washington, Esqr., dec'd, wch. she hath by devise of the sd. Henry Washington, dec'd, as may appear by the his will in the Court of Middlesex Co. afsd. wch. is hereafter conveyed and also in consideration of the sum of 5 shillings by the sd. Charlotte on behalf of herself and the afsd. Jane, Agnes and Mary, paid to Thacker Washington bef. the sealing and delivery of these Presents. The sd. Thacker hath granted , sold and confirmed unto the sd. Charlotte Neilson, and to her assigned during her natural life and from and after her decease to the afsd. Jane, Agnes and Mary, being 250 a. of the Hampstead Tr. in Middlesex Co, on both sides of the main road leading to Urbanna, and bnd. as by a survey thereof made by Isaac Carlton, Surveyor. **And, to include also the Slaves, stocks and articles such as – Phil, Billey, Frank Sally, Drummond, Kate, Sam, Billey, Martha, Jemmey, Vaughan, Johnney, Vaughan with their Increase** and all the stock of horses, cattle, sheep, hogs now on the Hampstead plantation together with the Chariot, half of the Silver plate and all the furniture now in possession of the sd. Charlotte by the afsd. devise and the rents, profits,, etc. from the sd. land, Slaves, stocks and articles increase of the Slaves, all to the sd. Charlotte during her life and after her decease to the afsd. Jane, Agnes, and Mary Neilson, etc. Wits.: Wm. Curtis, Staige Davis, William Berry. Signed: Wm. Steptoe, Attorney in fact for Thacker Washington. Attached is a hand drawn survey with its metes and bounds of the property, by Isaac Carleton, Surveyor, dated 18 Dec 1787, for

252.5 a. in Middlesex Co., in the fork of Washington's Mill Pond. 23 Jun 1788–
This Deed was recorded at Middlesex Co. Court House, Urbanna. – Will
Churchill.

Pg 81. 3 Jan 1788. Daniel Dejarnett and Elisabeth, his wife, of Hanover Co.,
VA, sells to John Healy, of Middlesex Co., VA for £140, for a piece of land in
Middlesex Co afsd., being the late property of John Meacham binding on land of
Hugh Walker, Benjamin Seward, Ben. Kidd, Carter Thurston, Susanna Daniel,
Benjamin [can't read last name], Mary Sheperd, being 120 a. Wits.: James Lee,
Thomas Patterson, Thomas Williams Saunders. Signed: Daniel Dejarnatt. 23
Jun 1788– This Deed was certified, and on 27 Oct 1788, the Deed was recorded
at Middlesex Co. Court House, Urbanna. – Will Churchill.

Pg 83. 25[?] Apr 1788. William Churchill and Elizabeth, his wife, [no
location] sell to George Blake, Junr.[no location], for £35, for a parcel of land in
the Parish of Christ Church, Middlesex Co., VA, for 30.5 a., beg. at a point on
the road that leads from Churchill's Mill to Urbanna, then to a point in
Brummil's line and then along same and then several courses to a point near the
road and then up same to the beg. Wits.: None. Signed: William Churchill.
Ackn.: 28 Jul 1788 – The Deed was recorded at Middlesex Co. Court House,
Urbanna. – Will Churchill.

Pg 84. 26 Jul 1788. Thomas Patterson, Middlesex Co., VA, sells to Tobias
Allen, of the afsd. place, for £5, for a tr. of land in the afsd. Co., being 5 a.
Wits.: Peter Montague, Isaac Carleton. Signed: Thomas Patterson. Ackn.: 28
Jul 1788 – The Deed was recorded at Middlesex Co. Court House, Urbanna. –
Will Churchill.

Pg 85. 25 Mar 1788. George Davis and Edmd. Berkeley, of Middlesex Co.,
VA, are firmly bound to Edmund Randolph, Esqr., and his [?] for £1,000. The
Condition is that sd. Davis was appointed Searcher at the Port of Urbanna and
that he truthfully perform his duties of the office concerning naval officers and
the collection of duties. Wits.: None. Signed: Geo. B. Davis, Edmd. Berkeley.
Ackn.: 23 Mar 1788 – The Bond was recorded at Middlesex Co. Court House,
Urbanna. – Will Churchill.

Pg 85. 9 Jan 1788. Henry Vass, Senr., of Middlesex Co., VA, sells to Thomas
Crittenden, John Daniel and James Lee, of the afsd. place, for £300, **for the
following Negroes – James, Abraham, Frank, Jone[?], Amand, Harry,
Milly[?], and Juday;** and also, 12 cattle, 4 horses, and household furniture.
Wits.: W. Segar, [FNU] Oliver. Signed: Henry Vass, Senr. Ackn.: 28 Jul 1788
– The Bill of Sale was recorded at Middlesex Co. Court House, Urbanna. – Will
Churchill.

Pg 86. 25 Feb 1788. Harry B. Yates, of the Parish of Christ Church, Middlesex Co., VA, for the good will and affection he bears **unto his dau. Sarah Yates, gives unto her a Negro girl named Anna, dau. of Jenny, a Slave.** Wits.: Samuel Klug, Cary Kemp. Signed: Harry B. Yates. Ackn.: 25 Feb 1788 – The Deed Poll was recorded at Middlesex Co. Court House, Urbanna. – Will Churchill.

Pg 86. 26 Apr 1788. James Baker, of Christ Church Parish, Middlesex Co., VA, sells to William Moore, of the afsd. place, for £64, 5 shillings, for 70 a., beg. at a corner of [can't read] Steptoe on the side of Mrs.[?] Millie Daniels' meadow swamp and then to the main Co. road, then along same to Mrs. Daniels land and then numerous courses to Mrs. Daniels' meadow fence and to the beg. Wits.: Christopher Garland, John Groom, Robert Groom. Signed: James G.[?] Baker. Ackn.: 28 Jul 1788 – The Deed was recorded at Middlesex Co. Court House, Urbanna. – Will Churchill.

Pg 87. 8 May 1788. John Daniel, of Middlesex Co., VA, for valuable consideration sells to Richard Street of the afsd. place, - **3 Negros named Jane, Billy, Fanny,** 2 feather beds, and furniture, 6 head of cattle, 1 table, 1 Lum[?], 1 spinning wheel, a pair of cards, and 1 sorrel mare. Wits.: Thomas Brook, Curtis Hady[Hardy?]. Signed: John Daniel. Ackn.: 8 May 1788 – The Deed Poll was recorded at Middlesex Co. Court House, Urbanna. – Will Churchill.

Pg 87. 1 Sep 1788. Thomas Turner and Catherine Turner, his wife, [no location] sell to William George [no location] for £39,1 shilling, 2 pence and further consideration of 5 shillings, for a certain piece of land in the Parish of Christ Church, Middlesex Co., VA, being 129 a., bnd. by land of Richard Corbin, Harry [B.?] Yates, Williamson Davis [?], Agrippa Dunn, Ann Gardner, James Lee and Benjamin Williams, Upon TRUST, nevertheless, that the sd. George shall after 10 Sep 1788, as soon as sd. George shall think proper shall sell for the best price for the land and premises, and the money from same to discharge and pay to William George the above sum of £39,1 shilling, 2 pence. with interest from 1 Sep 1788 until it is fully discharged. Wits.: James Lee, Jno. Henly[?], Overton Daniel. Signed: Thomas Turner, Catherine Turner, made her mark. Principal of within – 39.1.2, Sept 1, 1788; cash received 5.5.0,; balance due 33.6.2. Assigned the within to Francis Corbin, Esqr..- 25 Sep 1788 - W. George. Wits.: John George, Edward Ware. Ackn.: 27 Oct 1788 - The Deed of Trust from Thomas Turner and wife to William George and by sd. George assigned to Francis Corbin was recorded at Middlesex Co. Court House, Urbanna. – Will Churchill.

Pg 88. 27 August 1788. William Hill and Sarah, his wife, of Middlesex Co., VA, sells to John Jackson , of the afsd. place, for £119,1 shilling, 10 pence, for a piece of land in the Parish of Christ Church, in the afsd. state, being 132, 52 poles agreeable to the survey, beg. at a corner on the n. side of the main road in

John Boss's line and then numerous courses back to the beg. Wits.: None. Signed: William Hill, Sarah Hill. Ackn.: 27 Oct 1788 – The Deed was recorded at Middlesex Co. Court House, Urbanna. – Will Churchill.

Pg 90. 24 June 1788. William Churchill, of the Parish of Christ Church, Middlesex Co., VA, sells to Robert Spratt, of the afsd. place, for £255, 9 shillings, 11 pence, one half penny, for a tr. of land bot. by Armistead Churchill from Christopher Kibbee, by deed dated 2 Nov 1724, and lying in the afsd. Co., bnd. by the lands of sd. Churchill, being 500 a. and commonly known by the name of Kilbees, being a tr. of land and premises. Wits.: Jas. Ross, Geo. B. Davis, John Segar. Signed: None. Ackn.: 26 Jan 1789 – The Deed of Mortgage was recorded at Middlesex Co. Court House, Urbanna. – Will Churchill.

Pg 91. 23 Jun 1788. James Dunlevy and Edmund Berkeley are firmly bound unto Edmund Randolph, VA Gov., for £1,000. The Condition is that James Dunlevy was appointed Inspector of Tobacco at the Public Warehouse in Urbanna, Middlesex Co., VA, and that he shall faithfully fulfill his duties. Wits.: None. Signed: James Dunlevy, Edmd. Berkeley. Ackn.: 23 Jun 1788 – The Bond was recorded at Middlesex Co. Court House, Urbanna. – Will Churchill.

Pg 91. 26 Jan 1789. Clement Nicholson, of Middlesex Co., VA, and Ann, his wife, sell unto Hudson Muse, of the afsd. place, for £220, for a tr. of land in the afsd. place whereon sd. Nicholson and Ann, his wife, now live and commonly known as the Mickelborough Plantation, being 110a., wch. Clement Nicholson bot. from John Gordon and Lucy, his wife, by deed dated 1 Jun 1762. Wits.: Joseph Carter, Thomas Crittenden, Lawrence Moore. Signed: Clement Nicholson, Ann Nicholson. Ackn.: 26 Jan 1789 – The Deed was recorded at Middlesex Co. Court House, Urbanna. – Will Churchill.

Pg 93. 31 Aug 1787. Overton Cosby and James Gregory, surviving partners of James Mills & Co. sell to Overton Cosby's Company, of Urbanna, Middlesex Co., VA. WITNESSETH, that David Ker, by deed dated 17 Jun 1771, sold to James Mills & Co. one and one-half lot of land in the afsd. place, and whereas James Mills by a deed, dated 18 Jun 1771 sold to James Mills & Co., 2 lots; and also Overton Cosby and James Gregory are the surviving partners of James Mills & Co. NOW, THIS INDENTURE Witnesseth that Overton Cosby & James Gregory, as surviving partners, sell for £400 paid by Overton Cosby & Company, all the absd. lots sold and conveyed to James Mills & Co. by David Ker & James Mills, by their several & respective Indentures as absd; as they are numbered (on the Urbanna Town plan, dated 30 Jan.[?] 1747) 27, 28, & 29, and also one-half of lot(or quarter acre); bnd. n. by the public tobacco warehouse, e. by the Creek, s. by Virginia Street or the main street, & w. by Traffick lane, as the lane leading to fort point. Wits.: Ben Dabney, J.W.[?] Henry, Will Churchill, Staige Davis. Signed: Overton Cosby, Ja. Gregory. Ackn.: 26 Jan

1789 – The Deed was recorded at Middlesex Co. Court House, Urbanna. – Will
Churchill.

Pg 94. 1775. **Whereas, a sale was made betw. Philip Ludwill Grymes, of
Branden, Middlesex Co., VA, and John Randolph Grymes, then also of VA,
for sundry Negroes, to wit.: Robin, Pene, Philles, Bella, Jack, Venise[?,
Jenny, Beth[Bock?], Subey[?], Grace, Rose, Peg, Ben, Tom, Jenny, Dolly,
Cason[?], Bluff, Harry, Chris, Sally, Billy, Isabella, Scipia[?], Grace, Venus,
Tom, Bartswain[?], Tangion, Bob & Lucy- the afsd. Negroes being at the
afsd. period the property & in the possession of the afsd. John Randolph
Grymes. AND, WHEREAS, the sudden departure of the sd. John
Randolph Grymes, from VA and the late suspension of intercourse with
Great Britain & America, prevented compliance on the part of the sd. John
Randolph Grymes with the legal formalities for the establishment of
plenary right & indisputable title to the afsd. Negroes, in the afsd. Philip
Ludwell Grymes, KNOW ALL MEN by these Presents that I, John
Randolph Grymes do hereby sell to the sd. Philip Ludwell Grymes forever
all Right to & property in the absd. Negroes and in all present & future
Increase, and banning myself and claim to the sd. Negroes or their
offspring, present and future.** Wits.: M. Fauntt LeRoy, **London – 10 Feb
1787.** Signed: John R. Grymes. Ackn.: 26 Jan 1789 – The Bill of Sale was
recorded at Middlesex Co. Court House, Urbanna. – Will Churchill.

Pg 95. 22 Dec 1788. Staige Davis and Thomas Healy are firmly bound unto
Beverley Randolph, Esqr., Gov. VA, for £1,000. The Condition is that Staige
Davis was appointed hi Searcher at the Port of Urbanna and that he shall
faithfully perform the duties of his office. Wits.: Ja. Ross. Signed: Staige Davis,
Tho. Healy. Ackn.: 26 Jan 1789 – The Bond was recorded at Middlesex Co.
Court House, Urbanna. – Will Churchill.

Pg 95. 26 Jan 1789. NOW KNOW YE, that Clement Nicholson, and Anne, his
wife, of the Parish of Christ Church, Middlesex Co., VA, for and in
consideration of the Esteem and Good Will we have and do towards James Ross,
of the afsd. place**, have given and granted by these Presents, our Mulatto
woman Slave, Mary and her child, Nancy Woodford, with all their future
Increase, to have and to hold to James Ross, to his future use or uses and to
order and dispose of them at his and their Will and Pleasure.** Signed:
Clemt. Nicholson, Anne Nicholson. Wits.: Hudson Bird[?]. Ackn.: 26 Jan
1789 – The Deed of Gift was recorded at Middlesex Co. Court House, Urbanna.
– Will Churchill.

Pg 96. 26 Jan 1789. I, Clement Nicholson, of Middlesex Co., VA, have
appointed by these Presents Overton Cosby and James Ross, both of the afsd.
place, to be my true and lawful attorneys to do whatever in necessary in my
stead re: money, goods, wares, bonds, etc. And, to take possessions by all

lawful means whatsoever of all my Negroes, stocks, furniture and other things to me in my ways belonging, etc. Wits.: Hudson Muse[?], Staige Davis. Signed: Clemt. Nicholson. Ackn.: 26 Jan 1789 – The Power of Attorney was recorded at Middlesex Co. Court House, Urbanna. – Will Churchill.

Pg 97. 16[?] Jul 1788. John Robinson, of the Parish of Christ Church, Middlesex Co., VA, sells to Robert Spratt, of the afsd. place, for £69, 6 shillings, 10 pence, for a tr, of land whereon he now lives in the afsd. Co., bnd. by William Churchill, James Dunlevy and the Estate of Augustine Smith, being 414 a. Wits.: Overton Cosby, Geo. B. Davis. Signed: John Robinson. Ackn.: 26 Jan 1789 – The Deed of Mortgage was recorded at Middlesex Co. Court House, Urbanna. – Will Churchill.

Pg 98. 23 Apr 1789. I, Elizabeth Spotswood, of Middlesex Co., VA, sell to Col. William Churchill, for £355, for wch. I am justly indebted, the following **Slaves, to wit: Hannah, Fanny, Harry, Keziah, Menerva and Polly, and their future Increase,** and 40 head of black cattle, 20 head of hogs, 12 sheep unto the sd. William Churchill. Wits.: Peter Robinson, David Garland. Signed: Elizabeth Spotswood, made her mark. Ackn.: 17 Apr 1789 – The Bill of Sale was certified at Middlesex Co. Court House, Urbanna, and on 22 Jun 1789, the Bill of Sale was recorded at Middlesex Co. Court House, Urbanna. – Will Churchill.

Pg 98. 2 Nov 1788. Philip Warwick and Ann, his wife, of Lancaster Co., VA, sell to William Jessee, of Middlesex Co., VA, for £279, for a piece of land in the afsd. Co., being 205 a. including my mill. Wits.: James Lee, John Jessee, Overton Daniel. Signed: Philip Warwick, Ann Warwick. 27 Apr 1789 – The Deed was recorded at Middlesex Co. Court House, Urbanna. – Will Churchill.

Pg 99. 21 Nov 1788. Elizabeth Warwick, of Middlesex Co., VA, sells to William Jessee, for £100, my whole estate consisting of my Dower in the land and Mill, late the property of George Warwick, dec'd, and also my stock of cattle, horses, hogs and sheep, household and kitchen furniture. Wits.: John Mullins, Fras. Oliver, Alexd. Bristow. Signed: Elizabeth Warwick. 27 Apr 1789 – The Deed was recorded at Middlesex Co. Court House, Urbanna. – Will Churchill.

Pg 100. 13 Sep 1788. Nichols Tuggle [no location] sells to Thomas Healy [no location] for £29, 2 shillings, 7 pence, wch. the sd. Tuggle is justly indebted to the sd. Healy, and further pays 5 shillings to sd. Tuggle, for a tr. of land in the Parish of Christ Church, Middlesex Co., VA, being 23 a., bnd. by the lands of the sd. Healy and Thacker Washington and the Gray[?] Creek, UPON TRUST, nevertheless the sd. Healy shall after 1 Jan 1790, shall when the time is right or sd. Tuggle shall request, sell at the best price at public auction, and out of the money pay the afsd. £29, 2 shillings, 7 pence to satisfy the afsd. Healy, with interest from 13 Sep 1788 until the debt shall be discharged. Wits.; W. George, Henry Chowning, John Quarles. Signed: Nichols Tuggle. Ackn.: 17[?] Apr 1789 – The Deed of Trust was recorded at Middlesex Co. Court House, Urbanna. – Will Churchill.

Pg 102. 17 Apr 1789. I, Jonathan Denison, of Middlesex Co., VA, for diverse good causes and considerations, **have granted to William Denison, a Negro boy named Tom Lindsay and a Negro girl named Pol Lindsay, and to have and to hold the absd. Negroes to William Denison**, for his proper uses, etc. Wits.: George Walker, Wilkinson Barzey. Signed: Jonathan Denison. Ackn.: 28 Apr 1789 – The Deed of Gift was recorded at Middlesex Co. Court House, Urbanna. – Will Churchill.

Pg 102. 17 Apr 1789. I, Jonathan Denison, of Middlesex Co., VA, for diverse good causes and considerations, **have granted to Joseph Lewis Denison, a Negro boy named Sam Lindsay and a Negro girl named Fanny Lindsay, and to have and to hold the absd. Negroes to William Denison**, for his proper uses, etc. Wits.: George Walker, Wilkinson Barzey. Signed: Jonathan Denison. Ackn.: 28 Apr 1789 – The Deed of Gift was recorded at Middlesex Co. Court House, Urbanna. – Will Churchill.

Pg 103. 5 Nov 1788. Lawrence Meacham, of Middlesex Co., VA, sells to Maurice Smith, for £57, 2 shillings, 2 pence, wch. the sd. Meacham is justly indebted to sd. Smith, and in addition for the sum of 5 shillings, **for a Negro man Slave by the name of John,** UPON TRUST, and that the sd. Smith in 1789, as soon as sd. Smith shall think proper, or the sd. Meacham shall request of him to sell for the best price that can be gotten, the sd. Slave and Premises and out of the money arising to discharge to the sd. Smith the absd. £57, 2 shillings, 2 pence. Wits.: Thos. Healy, Wm. Curtis. Signed: L. Meacham. Ackn.: 28 Apr 1789[?] – The Deed of Trust was recorded at Middlesex Co. Court House, Urbanna. – Will Churchill.

Pg 104. 28[?] Dec 1788. William Moore of Middlesex Co., VA, sells to James Baker [no location], for £37, 7 shillings, 6 pence in gold & silver, for wch. the sd. Moore is justly indebted to the sd. Baker, and for the further consideration of 5 shillings, for a tr. of land now in possession of the sd. Moore, being 70 a., after 1 Nov 1790[?], or sooner, sell for the best price, and from the proceeds pay the £37, 7 shillings, 6 pence, with interest from 1 Nov 1790. Wit.: Wm. Nuscomb[?], Wm. Brown, made his mark, William Robinson. Signed: Wm. Moore, Thos. Patterson, Robert Groom, Thomas Groom, Peter Bray, made his mark. Ackn.: 28 Apr 1789[?] – The Deed of Trust was recorded at Middlesex Co. Court House, Urbanna. – Will Churchill.

Pg 105. 27 Apr 1789. George Daniel, and Frances, his wife, of Middlesex Co., VA, sell to James Healy, of the afsd. place, for £130, for a piece of land in the afsd. place, for 100 a., and also 42 a. of Dragon Swamp adj. the high land; beg. at John Wortham's line a little above his dwelling house at a point in the branch and then to a point on Ralph Wormeley's line and then along his line to the Dragon Run and then up same several courses back to the beg. , this land being part of land George Daniel bot. of Thomas Wortham with all houses, etc. Wits.: None. Signed: Geo. Daniel, Frances Daniel. Ackn.: 28 Apr 1789 – The Deed was recorded at Middlesex Co. Court House, Urbanna. – Will Churchill.

Pg 107. 3 Jun 1789. John Layton, and Mildred, his wife, of Middlesex Co., VA, sell to George West, of the afsd. place, for £29, for a parcel of land in the afsd. place, beg. at a point on the Gum[?] Branch Line at a ditch betw. Brummell, George, Blake and the sd. Layton and then running down same betw. Layton and Churchill, and then several courses to the head of the branch by Daniel Jefferson's and then numerous courses back to the beg., being 12 a.[?]. Wits.: Daniel Jefferson, George Blake, Junr., Thomas Clear[?]. Signed: John Layton, Maldread Layton. Ackn.: 26[?] Jun 1789 – The Deed was recorded at Middlesex Co. Court House, Urbanna. – Will Churchill.

Pg 108. 21 Apr. 1789. Thomas Segar, late Sheriff, of Middlesex Co., VA, sells to John Wake, Junr. of the afsd. place, at public sale, 29 a. in the Parish of Christ Church, Middlesex Co., for £6, 6 shillings, 7 pence, beg. at a point near the flowing water at the head of Shole Creek and then across to the other Creek below the house and landing of John Wake, dec'd, and then along the narrows, and then several courses to the beg. WHEREAS, Segar as Sheriff, exposed the land to public sale 29 a. that was part of the Estate of John Wake[?] , dec'd, to satisfy the public taxes due thereon. Wits.: Peter Kemp, John Quarles, Wilkenson Barzy, James Wortham. Signed: Thomas Segar. Ackn.: 22[?] Jun 1789 – The Deed was recorded at Middlesex Co. Court House, Urbanna. – Will Churchill.

Pg 110. 5 Jun 1789. Harry Beverley Yates, of Middlesex Co., VA, sells to Thomas Crittenden, of the afsd. place, for £150, for a parcel of land in the Parish of Christ Church, in the afsd. Co., being 200 a., beg. at a point in the Main Road, then s.e. to Corbin's line, then n.w. along his line to the n. side of the great Branch, and then done same to the mouth of Daniel's Spring Branch, and then up the Spring Branch, and then several courses to w. of Daniel's Road and then down same to Dejarnett's line, and then several courses to the beg. Wits.: B. Kidd, Junr., W. George, John Quarles, Benj. Kidd, Senr, made his mark. Signed: Harry B. Yates. Ackn.: 22 Jun 1789 – The Deed was recorded at Middlesex Co. Court House, Urbanna. – Will Churchill.

Pg 111. 31 Mar 1789. Doctor Robert Spratt, of Middlesex Co., VA, sells to Harry Beverley Yates, of the afsd. place, for £51, 12 shillings, 9 pence, for wch. the sd. Yates is indebted to the afsd. Spratt, and for another 5 shillings to the sd. Yates, does discharge and confirm to the sd. Spratt, **for the following 8 Slaves,**

92

to wit: **Anthony, Kitt, Frank, Jack, George, Billy, Nanny and Jenny, with their Increase,** UPON TRUST, where the sd. Spratt after 1 Jan 1790 to sell the said slaves and premises, and out of the money arising from the sale, will pay of £51, 12 shillings, 9 pence, plus interest from 31 Mar 1789. Wits.: Overton Cosby. Signed: Harry B. Yates. Ackn.: 26 Oct 1789 – The Deed of Trust was recorded at Middlesex Co. Court House, Urbanna. – Will Churchill.

Pg 112. 27 Oct 1789. John George, of Middlesex Co., VA, sells to William Gest and Mary, his wife [no location], for £129, 10 shillings, for 129.5 a., in the afsd. Co., per the survey by Isaac Carleton[?], on 2 Jul 1789, beg. at a point near the mouth of Cardwell's Sprint branch, corner to Mary Shepherd, then to a corner of Shepherd and Segougne, and then to a corner of George Bird and then several courses to Dragon Swamp, and then to a corner of Isaac Diggs and then up a run to a corner of John Seward and them along Seward's line, and then several courses back to the beg. Wits.: B. Kidd, Junr., Isaac Kidd, H. D. Shepherd. Signed: William Gest, Mary Gest made her mark. Ackn.: 26 Oct 1789 – The Deed was recorded at Middlesex Co. Court House, Urbanna. – Will Churchill.

Pg 114. 23 Sep 1789. Lunsford Daniel and Lydia, his wife, of Middlesex Co., VA, sell to Frances Oliver, of the afsd. Co., for £200, for a tr. of land in the sd. Co., beg. at the head of a Valley on the Mill Road and then along sd. Road to a line betw. Benj. Kidd, Senr. and John Healy, then e. to a corner of Meacham George and Daniel Stringer's land, and then along a line of Robert Thurston, dec'd and then to his corner and then to a fork of the branch and then down same to the Mill Dam, and then several courses to the beg., being 140 a. by estimation be the same more of less (**with the Grave Yards Exempted**). Wits.: N.[?] Daniel, Henry D. Shepherd, Mary Daniel, Susanna G. Daniel. Signed: Lunsford Daniel, Lydia Daniel. Ackn.: 26 Oct 1789 – The Deed was recorded at Middlesex Co. Court House, Urbanna. – Will Churchill.

Pg 116. 10 Sep 1789. William Churchill, and Elizabeth, his wife, of Middlesex Co., VA, sell to William Wood, of the afsd. place, for £250, for a piece of land in the afsd. Co., being 250 a., beg. on the e. side of a creek and then a course to Charles Dulus[?] line and then along same to the river, and then several courses back to the beg., and known as the Hardon's tract. Wits.: Edmd. Berkeley, Geo. Daniel, Francis Ross. Signed: Will Churchill, Elizabeth Churchill. 22 Oct 1789 – Edwd. Berkeley and George Daniel examined Elizabeth Churchill. Ackn.: 26 Oct 1789 – The Deed was recorded at Middlesex Co. Court House, Urbanna.

Pg 118. 28 Sep 1789. George Dilliard, and Mary, his wife, of Middlesex Co., VA, sell to Hudson Muse, Naval Officer, of Middlesex Co., for £130, for several tr. of land in Middlesex Co., on the main road to Urbanna, bnd. by land the afsd. Muse lately bot. from Clement Nicholson, the lands of William Steptoe, and Thacker Washington, Gent., being all the lands in the sd. tr. held by the sd.

Dilliard, wch. came by his Father, being 100 a. Wits.: Lawrence Muse, John
Roane, James Baker. Signed: George Dilliard, Mary Dilliard, made her mark.
Ackn.: 26 Oct 1789 – The Deed was recorded at Middlesex Co. Court House,
Urbanna – Will Churchill.

Pg 120. 25 Jan 1790. Lunsford Daniel, and Lydia, his wife, of Middlesex Co.,
VA, sell to Henry D. Shepherd, of the afsd. place, for £180, for land in the
Parish of Christ Church, in the afsd Co., for 180 a., beg. at the fork in the creek
and up the right to A[can't read] Gut, and the up same to William Jesse's line
and then to the road and to a corner of the afsd. Jesse and John Mullins and
James Ware, dec'd, then down to the head of Muddy Gut and down same to the
creek and then down same to the beg. Wits.: None. Signed: Lunsford Daniel,
Lydia Daniel. Ackn.: 26 Oct 1789 – The Deed was recorded at Middlesex Co.
Court House, Urbanna – Will Churchill.

Pg 121. 10 Feb 1789. Hugh Walker, and Catharine, his wife, of Culpepper Co.,
VA, sell to Louis Segougne, of the afsd. place, for £600, for a tr. of land in
Middlesex Co., VA, being with 4 other parcels annexed thereto 400 a.
(Neilson's, Saunders', Kidds, & Chowning's), lying on the Dragon Swamp,
Middlesex Co., with the main Dragon Run, the main body known by the name
of Meacham's Tract. Wit.: John T.[?] Walker, Robt. Holloway, Hetty[?]
Walker, Jane Denison. Signed: Hugh Walker, Catharine Walker. Ackn.: 28 Feb
1789 - John Waugh & Robt. Alcock, Magistrates of Culpepper Co., VA,
examined Catharine Walker. Wits: 24 Jan 1789 – William Churchill, Clerk.
Ackn.: 26 Oct 1789 – The Deed was recorded at Middlesex Co. Court House,
Urbanna – Will Churchill.

Pg 124. Receipt – Received of William Dudley £557, 4 shillings, 1 penny, in
full of all demands against the Exec. of William & Edwin Fleet. Wits.: Thos.
Moore. Signed: John Fleet. Ackn.: 25 Jan 1790 – The Deed was recorded at
Middlesex Co. Court House, Urbanna – Will Churchill.

Pg 124. 26 Oct 1789. Harry B. Yates, of Middlesex Co., VA, sells to Benjamin
Kidd, of the afsd. place, for £31, 10 shillings, for a tr. of land in the afsd. Co.,
being 35 a., beg. at a point on the n. side of the road from the Church to Ware's
Bridge and comes to Benjamin Kidd & Meacham George, then several courses
and then down the run of the branch and then numerous courses till it come to
the afsd. Kidd's corner and to the beg. Wits.: Warner Blake, H. George, Isaac
Carleton, John Thurston, Josiah Bristow, James Baker[?]. Signed: Harry B.
Yates. Ackn.: 28 Jun 1790 – The Deed was recorded at Middlesex Co. Court
House, Urbanna – Will Churchill.

Pg 125. 23 Jul 1789. Susanna Daniel, of Middlesex Co., VA, sells to Lunsford
Daniel of the afsd. place, for £65, wch. is for my part of my dec'd Father's land
lying in the afsd. place, being 65 a., and is bnd. by a tr. of land of William

Daniel, dec'd, of the afsd. place, by whose Will the sd. Susanna Daniel claims the afsd. land and apportionment of the land as by him, the sd. William Daniel, dec'd. And, she now conveys this land to the afsd. Lunsford Daniel, with all her Right of Dower. [According to the deed, she was paid £60, not £65, at the signing . Wits.: John Jackson, John Seward, Thos. Crittenden, N.[?] Daniel, H. D. Shepard, Wm. Shackelford. Signed: Susanna G. Daniel. Ackn.: 26 Oct 1789 – The Deed was recorded at Middlesex Co. Court House, Urbanna – Will Churchill.

Pg 127. 23 Jul 1789. Mary Daniel, of Middlesex Co., VA, sells to Lunsford Daniel of the afsd. place, for £65, wch. is for my part of my dec'd Father's land lying in the afsd. place, being 65 a., and is bnd. by a tr. of land of William Daniel, dec'd, of the afsd. place, by whose Will the sd. Mary Daniel claims the afsd. land and apportionment of the land as by him, the sd. William Daniel, defunct [dec'd?], bequeathed. And, she now conveys this land to the afsd. Lunsford Daniel, with all her Right of Dower. Wits.: John Jackson, John Seward, Thos. Crittenden, N. Daniel, H. D. Shepard, Wm. Shackelford. Signed: Susanna G. Daniel. Ackn.: 26 Oct 1789 – The Deed was recorded at Middlesex Co. Court House, Urbanna – Will Churchill.

Pg 129. 23 Sep 1789. Frances Oliver, and Ann, his wife, of Middlesex Co., VA, sell to Lunsford Daniel, of the afsd. place, for £200, for a tr. of land beg. at the fork of the creek running up the right prong to the mouth of Aecrey's[?] Gut, then up the gut to William Jessey's line, then to a corner to the road, then up same to a corner of William Jessee, John Mullins, and James Ware, dec'd[?], then down to the head of Muddy Gut and then down same to the creek and then to the beg., being 180 a. Wits.: N. Daniel, Henry D. Shepherd, Mary Daniel, Susanna G. Daniel. Signed: Francis Oliver, Ann Oliver, made her mark. Ackn.: 26 Oct 1789 – The Deed was recorded at Middlesex Co. Court House, Urbanna – Will Churchill.

Pg 130. 5 May 1789. Thomas Patterson, and Betsy, his wife, of Middlesex Co., VA, sell to Thomas Crittenden, of the afsd. place, for £150, for 312.75 a., lying in the Parish of Christ Church, in the afsd. Co., according to a survey made by Isaac Carlton on 9 Mar 1789, beg. at a corner of Tobias Allen and Henry Chowning and then several courses to a corner of the land sold for the mill binding on John George, and then to a point on Abbott's heirs, and then to a point on Robert Stamper[?] and then to a point binding on Brooks [can't read]. Wits.: William Chowning, Lawrence Muse, Henry Batchelder, George Dillard. Signed: Thomas Patterson, Elizabeth Patterson, made her mark. Ackn.: 26 Oct 1789 – The Deed was recorded at Middlesex Co. Court House, Urbanna – Will Churchill.

Pg 132. 14 May 1789. Overton Cosby and James Gregorie, surviving partners of James Mills & Co., of Middlesex Co., VA, of one part, and William Stiff, of the afsd. place, of the other part. Witnesseth, that for £193, 12 shillings, 5 pence, and wch. the sd. William Stiff is justly indebted to the afsd. Cosby and Gregorie, and desires to pay them back, and for the added sum of 5 shillings paid to sd. Stiff, and whereof the sd. Stiff, discharges the sd. Overton and Gregorie and **sells to them, a tr. of land on wch. the sd. Stiff now lives, being 491 a., bnd. by lands of Col. Wm. Churchill, John Scrosby and Major John Robinson, dec'd[?] and the following 18 Slaves, to wit: Gabriel, Gabriel, Junr., Robin, Curtis, James, Ralph, Davey, Pompey (male Slaves) and Nanny, Frankey, Juno, Lucy, Sally, Jenney, Alice, Esther, Hannah, and Fanny (female Slaves) , with their future Increase** , forever to their proper use, UPON TRUST, and after 1 Jun 1790, to sell and get the best price that can be gotten, and to use the money arising from the sales to satisfy the absd. debt of £193, 12 shillings, 5 pence. Wits.: Wilkinson Barzey, Jas. Ross, John Segar. Signed: William Stiff. Ackn.: 26 Oct 1789 – The Deed of Trust was recorded at Middlesex Co. Court House, Urbanna – Will Churchill.

Pg 134. 27[?] Aug 1789. Overton Cosby and James Gregorie, surviving partners of James Mills & Co., of Middlesex Co., VA, of one part, and Charles Dudley, of the afsd. place, of the other part. Witnesseth, that for £98, 4 shillings, 7 pence, and wch. the sd. Charles Dudley is justly indebted to the afsd. Cosby and Gregorie, and desires to pay them back, and for the added sum of 5 shillings paid to sd. Dudley, and whereof the sd. Dudley, discharges the sd. Overton and Gregorie and **sells to them, a tr. of land whereon the sd. Dudley now lives being 2155 a., bnd. by lands of W. Churchill, Wm. Wood ad John Wake and the following Slaves – Bob, Harry & Abraham (male Slaves)** and 12 head of cattle, 2 horses an the premises, forever to their proper use, UPON TRUST, and after 1 May 1790, to sell and get the best price that can be gotten, and to use the money arising from the sales to satisfy the absd. debt of £98, 4 shillings, 7 pence. Wits.: Staige Davis, Jas. Ross, John Segar. Signed: Charles Dudley. Ackn.: 26 Oct 1789 – The Deed of Trust was recorded at Middlesex Co. Court House, Urbanna – Will Churchill.

Pg 135. 23 Dec 1789. **Nelson Daniel and Mary Shepherd, his Mother**, of Middlesex Co. VA, sell to Thomas Crittenden, for £400, for a tr. of land in the afsd. place, being 160 a., beg. at a point on the main run of the ---iry Swamp a little below the mill, then down the run to the main run of Dragon Swamp, then down the run to a corner and then to a corner near Seward's house and then to a corner of John Seward and John George and then to George's corner and then to the beg. Wit.: H. D. Shepherd, Lunsford Daniel, Allen Howard, Robt. Shepherd. Signed: N. Daniel, Mary Shepherd, made her mark. Ackn.: 25 Jan 1790 – The Deed was recorded at Middlesex Co. Court House, Urbanna – Will Churchill.

Pg 137. 29 Jul 1789. Overton Cosby and James Gregorie, surviving partners of James Mills & Co., of Middlesex Co., VA, of one part, and William Hackney, of

96

the afsd. place, of the other part. Witnesseth, that for £125, 17 shillings, 2
pence, and wch. the sd. Hackney is justly indebted to the afsd. Cosby and
Gregorie, and desires to pay them back, and for the added sum of 5 shillings
paid to sd. Hackney, the sd. Hackney discharges the sd. Overton and Gregorie
and **sells to them , all that tr. of land whereon the sd. Hackney now lives,
being 200 a., bnd. by the lands of John Miller, John Sutton, Philip L.
Grymes, and Dudley Vaughan, and the seven following Negro Slaves, to
wit.: James, Phill, Humphrey (male Slaves) and Philis, Daphne, Junia,
Jenny (femal Slaves), and their future Increase,** UPON TRUST, and after 1
Jan 1790, to sell and get the best price that can be gotten, and to use the money
arising from the sales to satisfy the absd. debt of £125, 17 shillings, 2 pence
Wits.: Jas. Ross, Wilkinson Barzey, Staige Davis. Signed: William Hackney.
Ackn.: 26 Oct 1789 – The Deed of Trust was recorded at Middlesex Co. Court
House, Urbanna – Will Churchill.

Pg 139. 26 Oct 1789. John George, Junr., of Middlesex Co., VA, sells to
Lunsford Daniel, and Lydia, his wife, for £2, 4 shillings, for 6 a. of land, beg. at
a corner of sd. Lunsford Daniel and then several courses to a corner of John &
Benjamin Seward, and then a course to the beg. Wits.: N. Daniel, Wm.
Bowden, Thos. Mountague. Signed: Lunsford Daniel, Lydia Daniel. Ackn.: 26
Oct 1789 – The Deed was recorded at Middlesex Co. Court House, Urbanna –
Will Churchill.

Pg 140. 5 Sep 1789. George Blackley, and Molly, his wife, of Middlesex Co.,
VA, sell to Benjamin Kidd, Senr., of the afsd. place, for £100, for a piece of land
in the sd. Co., being 100 a., bnd. by lands of Benjamin Seward, Benjamin
Williamson, George Saunders' heirs, James Kidd, and the heirs of George
Saunders on the Dragon. Wits.: Jno. Healy, Kenny Kidd. Signed: George
Blackley, Molly Blackley. Ackn.: 26 Oct 1789 – The Deed was recorded at
Middlesex Co. Court House, Urbanna – Will Churchill.

Pg 141. 24 Oct 1789. James Baker, and Joanna, his wife, of Middlesex Co.,
VA, sell to Thomas Bray, of the afsd. place, for £45, for a tr. of land in the afsd.
place, bnd. by lands of Maurice Smith and Daniel, Robinson, [can't read] being
40 a. Wits.: Lenard Bristow, Rich. Bristow. Signed: James Baker, Joanna
Baker. Ackn.: 26 Oct 1789 – The Deed was recorded at Middlesex Co. Court
House, Urbanna – Will Churchill.

Pg 142. 21 Oct 1789. Daniel Stringer, Senr., of the Parish of Christ Church,
Middlesex Co, VA, for the natural love and affection wch. I have toward
William Stringer, my son, and also for good causes and other considerations,
grant to the sd. William Stringer the goods & chattels and **1 Negro woman
Slave, named Sally,** also a bed and furniture – first choice, and 3 grown cattle,

one-third of the stock of hogs, 6 chairs, 6 pewter plates, 1 dish, 1 chest, 1 spice mortar & pestle, 1 Dutch oven to him & his heirs forever at my decease whatsoever moveable, etc. as well as what is in my custody wherever including in the hands of other persons. Wits.: N. Daniel, Robert Chowning, Jacob Abbott, W. George. Signed: Daniel Stringer. Ackn.: 26 Oct 1789 – The Deed of Gift was recorded at Middlesex Co. Court House, Urbanna – Will Churchill.

Pg 143. 17 Oct 1789. Harry Beverley Yates, of Middlesex Co., VA, sells to John Quarles, of the afsd. place, for £45, 3 shillings, 2.5 pence, and also for 5 shillings, sells to sd. Quarles, a tr. of land in the afsd. place, adj. the lands of Benjamin Kidd, Senr., and the lands of George Saunders, lately dec'd, and those of Robert Chowning, and wch. land the afsd. Yates bot. of Isaac Ware, being 100 a., (except that the White Oak Swamp is not included) UPON TRUST and after 18 Oct 1789, for the sd. Quarles to sell the above 100 a. and premises and to pay off the debt of £45, 3 shillings, 2.5 pence with interest from the proceeds. Wits.: Robert Wattson, made his mark, John Murray. Signed: Harry B. Yates. Ackn.: 28 Jan 1790 – The Deed of Trust was recorded at Middlesex Co. Court House, Urbanna – Will Churchill.

Pg 145. 27[?] Oct 1789. Daniel Stringer, Senr., of Middlesex Co., VA, grants to Daniel Stringer, Junr., of Amelia Co., VA, for the natural love and affection wch. I have toward Daniel Stringer, Junr., my son, and also for good causes and other considerations, a tr. of land whereon I now live in Middlesex Co. afsd., being 200 a., and **also 1 Negro Slave, named Nanny [and/or?] Brandy Still** and all the plantation utensils, 4 chairs, 4 plates, 1 Bed & furniture, 1 pair of [can't read], 1 chest of drawers, 1 black walnut desk, 1 chest and other goods and chattels. Wits.: John George, N. Daniel, W. George, William Stringer. Signed: Daniel Stringer. Ackn.: 26 Oct 1789 – The Deed was recorded at Middlesex Co. Court House, Urbanna – Will Churchill.

Pg 146. 9 Jul 1789. Thomas Edgar, of the County of Middlesex, in Great Britain, appointed Anna Maria Edgar, to be his true and lawful attorney in his name and stead in America, regarding money, debts, etc. And, whereas, I have also nominated Philip Ludwell Grymes, Esqr., Middlesex Co., VA, attorney for the purposes afsd., and as the substitute for the sd. Anna Maria Edgar could do the above were I present and/or the sd. Grymes to be my substitute under this instrument. Signed: Anna Maria Edgar. Wits.: Wm. Gibson, Wm. Segar. Ackn.: 26 Oct 1789 – The Deed was recorded at Middlesex Co. Court House, Urbanna – Will Churchill.

Pg 147. 30[?] April 1790. Overton Cosby and Company, of the Town of Urbanna, Middlesex Co., VA, of one part and John Daniel, of the sd. Co., VA, of the other part. WITNESSETH, that for £21, 14 shillings, 1 penny of wch. John Daniel is justly indebted to the sd. Overton Cosby and Company, and for

5 shillings to John Daniel, sells to sd. Cosby, all that tr. of land whereon he now lives, being 200 a., adj. the lands of Frances Cloudas, James Jessee, Thomas Crittenden and Thomas Brooks[?], UPON TRUST that the sd. Overton after 1 Aug 1790 sells the land and from the money pay off the debt of £21, 14 shillings, 1 penny, with interest from 30 Apr 1790. Wits.: John Brooks, James Daniel, [can't read]. Signed: John Daniel. Ackn.: 28 Jun 1790 – The Deed of Trust was recorded at Middlesex Co. Court House, Urbanna – Will Churchill.

Pg 148. 4 Dec 1790. Levin Gale, of Somerset Co., MD, sells to Francis Corbin, of Middlesex Co., VA, for £1,527, 10 shillings, for land in Middlesex Co., VA, wherein the sd. Gale is now possessed, lying at the forks of a creek called and known as the Grange Creek, being 750 a. Wits.: Overton Cosby, John Segar, P. Kemp, Peter Kemp, Junr., Edward Lumpkin. Signed: Leven Gale. Ackn.: 27 Dec 1790 – The Deed was recorded at Middlesex Co. Court House, Urbanna – Will Churchill.

Pg 149. 4 Dec 1790. Leven Gale, of Somerset Co., MD, sells to Francis Corbin, Esqr., of Middlesex Co., VA, for £350, **11 Negro Slaves, to wit.: Will, Joe, Samuel, James, Buck, Lewis, Daniel, Robin, Hannah, Nanny, and Judith.** Wits.: Overton Cosby. Ackn.: 27 Dec 1790 – The Bill of Sale was recorded at Middlesex Co. Court House, Urbanna – Will Churchill.

Pg 149. 7 Apr 1790. Richard Corbin, of Laneville, Parish of Stratton Major, King & Queen Co., VA, Esq., sells to Francis Corbin, of Middlesex Co., VA, the son of the sd. Richard Corbin above, for the natural love and affection he bears toward his son, and also for the sum of $10, for all that Plantation tr. in Middlesex Co. afsd. and commonly known as Price's Plantation, being 1,180 a. together will the water grist mill adj. and usually occupied. **ALSO, the following Negroe Slaves and their future increase, to wit: Steptow, Somerset, Michael[?], Dick, Michael, Billy, Joshua, old Dick, and at the mill – Grace, Billy, Lilly, Angiler, Mary, Old Betty, Ganan[?], Toby, Jack, Jerey, Billy, Marsh, Butbridge[?], Harrison, Faney, Nancy, Phebey, Grace, Sukey, Lucy, Betty**. Also, 27 head of meat cattle, 5 horses, 14 sheep, 53 hogs. Wits.: John Taylor Corbin, Thos. Corbin, S.H. Henry. Signed: Rd. Corbin. Ackn.: 28 Jun 1790 – The Deed was recorded at Middlesex Co. Court House, Urbanna – Will Churchill.

Pg 150. 12 Feb 1789. Mary Blackburn, of the Parish of Christ Church, Middlesex Co., VA, lends for the consideration of the esteem and good will she bears unto her dau., Elizabeth Hodges, of the afsd. place, during her natural life the following: Cattle, 3 cows and 2 yearlings and all their future Increase, 1 bell metal skillet, 1 copper tea kettle, 5 silver teaspoons, 1 large table spoon, 1 pair of silver sugar tongs, and at her death, to be equally divided among all the

children she has or may have by John Hodges. AND, I, the sd. Mary Blackburn
do warrant and ever defend unto my sd. dau., Elizabeth Hodges the absd. items
and at the death of my dau., they are to be equally divided amongst all the
children she has or may have by John Hodges. Wits.: Sarah Webmore, John
Webmore. Signed: Mary Blackburn. Ackn.: 26 Oct 1789 – The Deed was
recorded at Middlesex Co. Court House, Urbanna – Will Churchill.

Pg 151. 20 Apr 1789. Thomas Segar, late Sheriff, of Middlesex Co., VA, sold
to Thomas Healy, of the afsd. place, for land he sold as Sheriff at public sale.
NOW, BY THIS INDENTURE, in consideration of the sum of £11, 5 shillings
from sd. Healy sells the 18 a. of land wch. is part of the Estate of Charles Reade,
dec'd, in the Parish of Christ Church, Middlesex CO. afsd., beg. at a point on the
w. side of the main road leading from Urbanna to James Kidd's and then to
Taylor's line, and then to a point in Washington's line, and then up the sd. road
to the beg. Wits.: Peter Kemp, John Quarles, Wilkinson Barzey, James
Wortham. Signed: Thomas Segar. Ackn.: 26 Oct 1789 – The Deed was
recorded at Middlesex Co. Court House, Urbanna – Will Churchill.

Pg 152. 8 May 1789. Maurice Smith, of Middlesex Co., VA, sells to John
Smith, of the City of Williamsburg, VA, for £150, for 200 a. of land in
Middlesex Co., beg. on the line at the lower extreme of my land adj. the land
form. called Jones Tract on the one side adj. the land of Wm. Murray's[?] heirs
on the other side. Wits.: None. Signed: Maurice Smith. Ackn.: 26 Oct 1789 –
The Deed was recorded at Middlesex Co. Court House, Urbanna – Will
Churchill.

Pg 153. 28 Sep 1789. William Roane, of the Parish of Christ Church,
Middlesex Co., VA, sells to Josiah Bristow, of the afsd. place, for £44[?], 1
shilling, for 44.5 a., beg. at a point on side of [can't read] Swamp, then up same
to the fork of the swamp and then Thacker's Spring Branch and then to the beg.
Wits.: Peter Bray, made his mark, Nancy Emberson, made her mark, Jno.
Roane, Richd. Bristow, Cary Kemp, Thomas Bray. Signed: Wm. Roane.
Ackn.: 26 Oct 1789 – The Deed was recorded at Middlesex Co. Court House,
Urbanna – Will Churchill.

Pg 154. 14 Oct 1789. I, here certify to the Middlesex Co., VA Court, that I
have this day settled all accounts and demands with Mr. William Jackson, for
his engagements as my Guardian and do here by ackn. to have received full
satisfaction of him and I discharge him for all his actions and doings as afsd..
Wits.: James Quarles, William Berry. Signed: James Batchelder.
Ackn.: 27 Oct 1789 – The Receipt was recorded at Middlesex Co. Court
House, Urbanna – Will Churchill.

Pg 154. 25 Jan 1790. James Healy, of Middlesex Co., VA, and, Ruth, his wife, sell to Ralph Wormeley, Junr., of the afsd. place, for £130, for a piece of land in the afsd. place, being by survey 100 a. of high land, and also 42 a. of Dragon Swamp adj. the sd. high land, beg. at John Wortham's line a little above his dwelling house, at a point in the branch on the afsd. Wormeley's line and then along same to the Dragon Run and then up the side of the run to the beg. AND, the land is part of the land wch. George Daniel bot. of Thomas Wortham. Wits.: Edmd. Berkeley, Skelton Murray, Will Churchill. Signed: James Healy, Ruth Healy, made her mark. Ackn.: 25 Jan 1790 – The Deed was recorded at Middlesex Co. Court House, Urbanna – Will Churchill.

Pg 156. 15 Oct 1789. James Quarles, and Mary, his wife, [no location], sell to William Jackson, of Middlesex Co., VA, for £83, for a tr. of land on the Rapahanock River, in the Parish of Christ Church, Middlesex Co. VA, wch. is the balance of a larger tr. sold to William, and his brother, John Jackson, and commonly called and known by the name of Pine Top, as by a survey made by Isaac Carlton, being 83 a., beg. at the mouth of a cove of Little Oyster Creek, and then to a corner of John Jackson and then to a corner of William Jackson and then numerous courses to the head of a branch of Broad Creek and then down the sd. Creek to the Rapahanock River, and up the river as it meanders to the mouth of Little Oyster Creek, and then up the sd. Creek to the beg. Wits.: John Sutton, George Jackson, William Berry, Alex. Anderson. Signed: James Quarles, Mary Quarles. On 5 Dec 1789, James Hill and Isaac Quarles examined Mary Quarles. Ackn.: 25 Jan 1790 – The Deed was recorded at Middlesex Co. Court House, Urbanna – Will Churchill.

Pg 157. 30 May 1789. Louis De Segougne, and Julie, his wife, of Middlesex Co., VA, sell to Hugh Walker, of Culpepper & Anthony Gardner, of the County of King & Queen, VA, for £600, for a parcel of land in Middlesex Co. afsd., being 400 a., being the tr. of land bot. from Hugh Walker and whereon I presently live, the main body form. bot. by the afsd. Walker from John Meacham. Wit.: Thomas Segar, Wm. Bowden, John T. Walker. Signed: Louis Sigougne, Julie Segougne. 25 Jan 1790 – The Deed was proved by the Oath of Thomas Segar. And, on 25 Apr 1791 – The Deed was proved by the Oath of William Bowden and certified at Middlesex Co. Court House, Urbanna – Will Churchill.

Pg 159. 4 Dec 1789. Elliott Sturman, and Mary, his wife, of Essex Co., VA, sell to Hudson Muse, of Middlesex Co., VA, for £485, for all those lots in Urbanna, Middlesex Co., VA, wch. Sturman bot. from Hugh Walker and Catharine, his wife by deed, dated 17 Nov 1784. Wits.: George Dame, John Mickelburrough, Will Steptoe, Thomas Iverson. Signed: Elliott Sturman, Mary Sturman. Ackn.: 25 Jan 1790 – The Deed was recorded at Middlesex Co. Court House, Urbanna – Will Churchill.

Pg 160. 11 Jan 1790. Lunsford Daniel, and Lydia, his wife, of Middlesex Co., VA, sell to Thomas Crittenden, of the afsd. place, for £146, 10 shillings, for apiece of land in the afsd. Co., beg. at a corner of Nelson Daniel, and then to a corner of John George and then to a corner of sd. George and Benjamin Seward's line, and then several courses to the main road and then a course to the head of Nalley Corner, and then to Francis Oliver, and then down an irregular line to the Mill and then to the Mill Pond; bnd. by natural high lands and low ground to the Mill House and then down the run to Nelson Daniel's line, and then a few courses to the beg., being 77.5 a. ALSO, the aforementioned Mill and all its appurtenances and to hold the precious acreage together with 2 a. of land adj. the lands of Thomas Segar and John Jackson and belonging to the Mill. Wits.: None. Signed: Lunsford Daniel, Lydia Daniel. Ackn.: 25 Jan 1790 – The Deed was recorded at Middlesex Co. Court House, Urbanna – Will Churchill.

Pg 161. 31 Oct 1789. Daniel Stringer, the Elder, of the Parish of Christ Church, Middlesex Co., VA, of one part and Philip Mountague, and John George, Gent., of the other part. WITNESSETH, that Daniel Stringer, the Elder, in consideration of several uses and trusts hereafter to be mentioned and expressed and for the sum of 5 shillings paid to sd. Stringer, who sells unto them of the other party or the Survivor of them**, the following Negro Slaves and their Increase, that is to say – Jane, Hampton, Hanna, Bristow, Fortune or Forten, Mill, Sarah, and Mary or Moll.** ALSO, the following stock and their Increase – 2 horses (one Bay and one Sorrel horse), 9 cattle, 2 feather beds, and furniture, 6 chairs, 6 plates, IN TRUST, nevertheless and for the several uses and trusts following – IN TRUST, that they stand possessed of the absd. Negro Slaves and other items**. AND, IN TRUST, possessed of one Slave named Jane and all her Increase for the use of his, the sd. Daniel Stringer's dau., Caroline Hughs, and her Increase forever, and also IN TRUST that they will stand possessed of 1 feather bed and furniture, 6 chairs, 6 plates in trust for the use of the sd. Caroline Hughes. IN TRUST, they stand possessed of the Negro Slaves Hampton and Hannah and all their future Increase for the use of Fanny Chowning, the wife of Robert Chowning, but upon the Condition nevertheless that they the sd. Fanny Chowning and Robert Chowning relinquish and transfer to the sd. Mountague and George all of their (the sd. Fanny & Robert, their Right Property Claim, Demand, Estate, wch. they or any other gift from sd. Stringer, the Elder, in) – to the Slave Sarah.** And, IN FURTHER TRUST, the sd. Mountague and the sd. George, shall stand possessed of all the rest of the residue of the estate to wit.: the **Negro Slaves, horses, etc. for the use of Daniel Stringer, Junr. & William Stringer, for the purpose of paying and satisfying all such just claims and demands against the sd. Daniel Stringer, the Elder.** AND, THAT, LASTLY IN TRUST, after the payment of all such debts, etc. they will stand possessed of the residue of the estate for the use and benefit of the sd. Daniel Stringer, Junr., William Stringer, and Caroline Hughes forever, and to be

divided equally betw. them. Wits.: W. George, Wm. Owen, John Wortham.
Signed: Daniel Stringer. Ackn.: 25 Jan 1790 – The Deed of Trust was recorded
at Middlesex Co. Court House, Urbanna – Will Churchill.

Pg 163. 11 Jul 1789. Articles of Agreement. **William Crittenden Webb, of
Orange Co., VA, of the one part, and Fanny Wortham, widow and relict of
James Wortham, dec'd, of Middlesex Co., VA, who will shortly, as
intended, solemnize and hold a Marriage betw. them.** These Articles are in
consideration of the intended marriage and the afsd. Webb does agree to lend to
the afsd. Wortham, a child's part of all his Estate in Orange Co., provided that
she, the sd. Fanny Wortham shall outlive him for and during her natural life and
no longer wch. child's part is to be in lieu of her Dower. **AND, whatever
Estate the sd. Fanny Wortham may have at the time of her intermarrying,
wch. the sd. William Crittenden Webb or whatever Estate her father, Coll.
Maurice Smith may give the sd. Fanny,** the sd. William Crittenden Webb is to
enjoy it for and during his natural life and after his death to return to the sd.
Fanny to be disposed off as she shall think proper. Wits.: Samuel Klug, John
Shelton. Signed: Wm. C. Webb, Fanny Wortham, made her mark. Ackn.: 25
Jan 1790 – The Articles of Marriage were certified at Middlesex Co. Court
House, Urbanna – Will Churchill.

Pg 163. 26 Apr 1790. William Churchill, of Middlesex Co., VA, and Elizabeth,
his wife, sell to John Wake, of the afsd. Co., for £83, for a tr. of land in the
Parish of Christ Church, Middlesex Co., being 83 a.; beg. at a corner of
Batchelder and then to a point near the school house, and then to a corner of
Churchill in Charles Dudley's line, and then along same to a corner of Ambrose
Wake, and then several course to the beg. Wits.: Ralph Wormeley, Junr.,
Francis Corbin, Edmd. Berkeley. Signed: William Churchill, Elizabeth
Churchill. Ackn.: 26 Apr 1790 – The Deed was recorded at Middlesex Co.
Court House, Urbanna – Will Churchill.

Pg 165. 29 Sep 1789. John Scrosby, Simon Laughlin, and Ann, his wife, of the
Parish of Christ Church, Middlesex Co., VA, sell to John Roane, of the afsd.
place, for £900, for a tr. of land in the afsd. place, being 900 a., beg. at the n. end
of Gray's Point running along the river shore to the mouth of Mitchem's [?]
Creek, then s. up to the head of the Creek to a point in Willow branch, wch. is a
line tree by Major William Stiff and the sd. John Scrosby, then e. along Stiff's
line, then along Mrs. Elizabeth Wake's line to a ditch, then along same down to
the Creek, then along Island Shore across Back Creek to the beg., including all
the land on the e. side of Mitchem's Creek. Wits.: W. Segar, Wm. Curtis, John
Scrosby, Simon Laughlin, Ann Laughlin, Robert Matthews, John Miller. 22 Apr
1790 – Macham Boswell, Armistead Smith examined Ann Laughlin. Ackn.: 26
Apr 1790 – The Deed was recorded at Middlesex Co. Court House, Urbanna –
Will Churchill.

Pg 167. 28 Mar 1790. Paulin Anderson Blackburn, of the Parish of Christ Church. Middlesex Co., VA, sells to David Garland [no location], for £40, 17 shillings, for a parcel of land in the afsd. place, being 43 a. lying betw. the 2 main rods leading from the lower Chappel to Eliott's Warehouse and Seaton's Ferry joining a piece of land now of Charles Grymes, Esqr. and Coll. Edmund Berkeley, wch. land of the sd. Berkeley was form. that of Edward Blackburn called Coopper's old field above the land. Wits.: John Hodges, Coveil Blad, John Jackson, Junr. Signed: Paulin Blackburn. Ackn.: 26 Apr 1790 – The Deed was recorded at Middlesex Co. Court House, Urbanna – Will Churchill.

Pg 168. 16 Dec 1789. Thacker Washington, and Harriet, his wife, of King George Co., VA, sells to Hudson Muse, of Middlesex Co., VA, for £1,000, for a tr. of land in Middlesex Co afsd., abt. 3 miles from Urbanna and known by the name of Hampstead, being 752 a., with a mill and all the improvements thereon, wch. land came by his Father, the late Henry Washington, dec'd, and is all the lands that the sd. Thacker and his wife, Harriet, held in Middlesex Co. Wits.: Elliott Sturman, Jas. Ross, Staige Davis, Thomas Crittenden, P. Kemp. Signed: Thacker Washington, Harriet Washington. 2 Feb 1790 - George Fitzhugh and Burditt Ashton examined Harriet Washington. Ackn.: 26 Apr 1790 – The Deed was recorded at Middlesex Co. Court House, Urbanna – Will Churchill.

Pg 171. 1 Nov 1789. Milly Daniel, Guardian of Lucy Daniel, orphan, of the Parish of Christ Church, Middlesex Co., VA, of one part and Ann Curtis, of the afsd. place, of the other part. And, the sd. Milly Daniel for the consideration of the yearly rent hath granted unto Ann Curtis all the messuage and tenement in the afsd. place (known by the name of Batchelder's) from the afsd. date for & until her dau., Lucy Daniel comes of age or married, and fully to be paying therefore yearly during the sd. term unto Milly Daniel the yearly rent of £11 or in tobacco at the Market Place at the option of the payer, on or bef. 1 Jan in each year or any part to be behind & unpaid in the space of 20 days. Also, the sd. Curtis shall make reasonable repairs in the dwelling house and shall build a stable 24 feet by 20 feet, and a barn house that shall contain 120 barrels, and the value of the absd. repairs and building shall be taken out of the rent.. Also, the sd. Curtis shall clear 15 a. and shall have all the firewood. Wits.: John Curtis, Jno. Roane, Thos. Healy, W. Segar. Signed: Milly Daniel. Ackn.: 28 Jun 1790 – The Deed of Lease was recorded at Middlesex Co. Court House, Urbanna – Will Churchill.

Pg 172. 28 Dec 1789. James Bristow, and Molley, his wife, of Gaits Co., NC; and Bartholomew Bristow, and Nancy his wife; and Josiah Bristow, and Fanny, his wife, of Middlesex Co., VA, sell to James Healy, of Middlesex Co., VA, for £400, for a tr. of land in Middlesex Co., VA, being 100 a.; bnd by the lands of Benjamin Bristow's heirs, Robert Murray's heirs, John South & Ralph Wormeley, Esqr., John Healy, Henry Kidd, Micham Wortham, made his mark. Signed: James Bristow, Bartholomew Bristow, Nancy Bristow, made her mark,

Josiah Bristow, Fanny Bristow. Ackn.: 28 Jun 1790 – The Deed was ordered to be recorded. 27 Dec 1790, this Deed was recorded at Middlesex Co. Court House, Urbanna – Will Churchill.

Pg 174. 28 Jun 1790. Benjamin Seword, of Middlesex Co., VA, and Ann, his wife, sell to John Healy, of the afsd. place, for £61, for a parcel of land in the afsd. place, being 55 a., beg. at a point in the White Oak Swamp cornering on Carter Huston's Orphan's land, and bnd. by the sd. Orphan's land along a line and then cornering on the sd. Orphan's land and John Healy, and then along the line of Healy, and then several courses to Benjamin Kiid, Senr.'s and then to the beg., and it was a piece of land that Benjamin Seword bot. from John George, Junr. Wits.: None. Signed: Benjamin Seward, Anne Seward. Ackn.: 28 June 1790 – The Deed was recorded at Middlesex Co. Court House, Urbanna – Will Churchill.

Pg 175. Jan 1790. William Owen, of Middlesex Co., VA, of one part and Harwood Burt, of York Co., VA, of the other part. WITNESSETH, for 5,867 pounds of crop tobacco and interest and also for £2, 10 shillings, 10 pence, one-half penny, wch. the sd. William Owen is justly indebted to the sd. Harwood Burt, desires to pay his debt. **Therefore, the sd. Owen for 5 shillings to him, sells to sd. Burt forever – 1 Negroe Slave (Man) Nathaniel, 1 (Woman) Eleanor, and Lucy, Abraham, Beverly, UPON TRUST, and sd. Burt, after 1 Dec 1790, Burt shall sell the sd. Slaves and other premises and to take out the money arising from same to pay and satisfy the debt of the 5,860 pounds of crop tobacco and also for £2, 10 shillings, 10 pence, one-half penny, with interest from 7 Jan 1790, until the debt is discharged.** Wit.: Wm. Bowden, W. Segar, Staige Davis, W. George. Signed: Wm. Owen. Ackn.: 28 Jun 1790 - The Deed of Trust was recorded at Middlesex Co. Court House, Urbanna – Will Churchill.

Pg 177. 26 Dec 1789. William Owen, and June, is wife, of Middlesex Co., VA, sell to Ralph Watts [no location], for £41, 10 shillings, for a parcel of land in the afsd. Co., binding on John Watts, beg. at a point in John Watts' line and then several courses to John Jackson's line and then along same to a branch of the Briney Swamp and then down the run of same to a corner of the absd. Jackson and in Robert Daniel's line, and then along same to a point in the afsd. Swamp and then to a point near Owen's fence and then to the beg., being 41.5 a. Wits.: G. Bird, Thomas Segar, Jno. Healy. 9 Feb 1790 - Will Churchill directed G. Bird and Thomas Segar to examine June Owen. 17 Feb 1790 – G. Bird and Thomas Segar examined June Owen. Ackn.: 28 Jun 1790 - The Deed was recorded at Middlesex Co. Court House, Urbanna – Will Churchill.

Pg 179. 28 Jun 1790. Leonard George, John Quarles and William George are firmly bound unto Beverley Randolph, Gov. of VA, for £1,000. The Condition is that Leonard George shall faithfully execute his office as Surveyor for

Middlesex Co.. Wits.: None. Signed: Leonard George, John Quarles, W. George. Ackn.: 28 Jun 1790 - The Bond was recorded at Middlesex Co. Court House, Urbanna – Will Churchill.

Pg 179. 28 Jun 1790. Wm. Hackney, Thos. Healy and Thos. Churchill are held and firmly bound unto Beverley Randolph, Gov. of VA, for £1,000. The Condition is that William Hackney faithfully execute the duties of his office as Inspector of Tobacco at the public warehouse. Wits.: None. Signed: Wm. Hackney, Thos. Healy, Thomas Churchill. Ackn.: 28 Jun 1790 - The Bond was recorded at Middlesex Co. Court House, Urbanna – Will Churchill.

Pg 180. 28 Jun 1790. Thomas Crittenden, and Jane, his wife, of Middlesex Co., VA, sell to Lunsford Daniel, of the afsd. place, for £205, for a tr. of land in the afsd. place, being 205 a., it being form. the land of Henry B. Yates, dec'd, late of the afsd. Co., and is bnd. by lands of Richard Corbin, Thomas Turner, William Davis and the aforementioned Henry B. Yates' orphan's land, beg. near the main county road and then to Corbin's line and then along same to the n. side of the great branch, and then down the main run of the branch to the mouth of Turner's Spring Branch, and then up the Spring Branch to a point near the head, and then to Turner's road and then down same to Turner's corner by the road, then along Turner's line to William Davis' corner near the main road and then down the sd. road to the beg. Wits.: None. Signed: Thos. Crittenden, Ganey Crittenden. Ackn.: 28 Jun 1790 - The Deed was recorded at Middlesex Co. Court House, Urbanna – Will Churchill.

Pg 181. 28 Jun 1790. Thomas Crittenden, and Jane, his wife, of Middlesex Co., VA, sell to John Jackson of the afsd. place, for £170, 6 shillings, for a tr. of land in the afsd. Co., wch. was part of a tr. of land bot. by Thomas Crittenden from Nelson Daniel and Mary Shepherd, his mother, as by deed, dated 23 Dec 1789, being 131 a., beg. at a point on the s. side of Briery Run close to the Mill Tail, then along a line to a corner of Benjamin Seward's, then and along a line to John Seward, Senr.'s line close by his apple orchard, and then to a point in the line of John Seward's, and then along a line to the main road of the Dragon Swamp, and then up same to the main run of sd. Dragon Swamp to the main run of the Briery Swamp and then up the run to the beg. Wits.: None. Signed: Thos. Crittenden, Ganey Crittenden. Ackn.: 28 Jun 1790 - The Deed was recorded at Middlesex Co. Court House, Urbanna – Will Churchill.

Pg 183. 28 Jun 1790. Richard Davis, Benjamin Hackney and Staige Davis are firmly bound unto Beverley Randolph, Esqr., Gov. of VA, for the sum of £1.000. The Condition is that Richard Davis is appointed Inspector of Tobacco at the public warehouse at Kemp's, Middlesex Co., VA and that he faithfully performs the duties of his office. Wits.: None. Signed: Richard Davis, Benjamin Hackney, Staige Davis. Ackn.: 28 Jun 1790 - The Bond was recorded at Middlesex Co. Court House, Urbanna – Will Churchill.

Pg 184. 27 Aug 1789 – Court Order. Agreeable to an Order of the Middlesex Co. Court, VA, we John Daniel & Churchill Blakey, do agree to submit all maters is dispute betw. them re: a certain parcel of land to be determined by John George, Senr., Thomas Healy, Francis Corbin and Overton Cosby, Gent., or any three of them and their award to be final, and I, John Daniel do covenant and agree to mortgage my land in sd. Co., form. the land of the sd. Blakey, being 200 a, with all things thereto belonging to Churchill Blakey to satisfy the sd. Blakey, the damages that may be found by the sd. arbitrators against me in favor of the sd. Blakey. In Witness hereof, we have set our hands and seals this date. Wits.: B. Kidd, James Wortham, John Brooks. Signed: John Daniel, Churchill Blakey. Ackn.: 24 Jan 1795 - The Articles of Agreement were recorded at Middlesex Co. Court House, Urbanna – Will Churchill.

Pg 184. 29 Oct 1789. I, Daniel Stringer, of Middlesex Co. VA, for and in consideration of the love, goodwill and affection, wch. I have and do bear towards my dau., Sarah Abbott, of King & Queen Co., VA**, I have granted by these Presents, give her - 2 Negro, viz. arniggo Woman by the name of Aggy, her son, Bob, of wch. (bef. the signing of these Presents I have delivered her to the sd. Sarah Abbott, to have and to hold the sd. Negros to her the sd. Sarah Abbott, her heirs, etc. from henchforth as her and their proper Slaves without any manner of Condition.** Wits.: William Kidd, made his mark, Robert Chowning. Signed: Daniel Stringer. Ackn.: 28 Jun 1790 - The Deed of Gift was recorded at Middlesex Co. Court House, Urbanna – Will Churchill.

Pg 185. 29 Oct 1789. **I have delivered her, the sd. Sarah Abbot, to have and to hold the sd. Negro to her, the sd. Sarah Abbot, her heirs, Exec., etc. from henceforth as her and their proper Slaves, absolutely without any manner of Condition.** Wits.: William Kidd, made is mark, Robert Chowning. Signed: Daniel Stringer, made his mark. Ackn.: 28 Jun 1790 - The Deed of Gift was recorded at Middlesex Co. Court House, Urbanna – Will Churchill.

Pg 185. __ Oct 1789**. I, Andrew Davis, of Middlesex Co., VA, have freely granted unto my dau., Elizabeth Davis, of the afsd. place, for the love and affection I bear unto her, 1 Negro boy named Carter, for her own proper use and behoof forever to keep or dispose of at her will & pleasure without any manner of challenge, claim or demand of me. And, I have put the sd. Sarah Davis in full possession of the afsd. Negro boy Carter.** Wits.: George Pasquet, John Woodley, made his mark, Geo. B. Davis. Signed: Andrew Davis. Ackn.: 28 Jun 1790 - The Deed Poll was recorded at Middlesex Co. Court House, Urbanna – Will Churchill.

Pg 186. 4 May 1790. John Jackson and Cathrin, his wife, of Middlesex Co., VA, sell to Thomas Crittenden, of the afsd. place, for £41, 10 shillings, for a tr.

of land in the upper part of Middlesex Co., VA, beg. at a point in the line of sd. Crittenden & Betty Kemp, and then along a line to the mouth of a small branch, and then up same to the head of the branch and then to the line of John Secars[Segar's] and along same to Henry Vass's and to sd. Crittenden's line and then to the beg., being 41.5 a. Wits.: Thomas Segar, W. Segar, Thos. Segar, Junr. Signed: John Jackson, Catharine Jackson. Ackn.: 28 Jun 1790 - The Deed was recorded at Middlesex Co. Court House, Urbanna – Will Churchill.

Pg 187. 2 Jan 1790. William Curtis, Middlesex Co., VA, of the one part and Harwood Birt, of York Co, VA, of the other part. WITNESSETH, that William Curtis for £300 to him paid by sd. Birt and by these Presents confirms unto the sd. Birt all that tr. of land lately bot. from the afsd. Birt by William Curtis, being in Middlesex Co. afsd., and the reversion and remainder with all estate Right to the sd. land, to have and to hold the afsd. land and premises unto the sd. Birt forever. Provided nevertheless and it is hereby agreed betw. the parties if these Presents that if the sd. William Curtis or Charles Curtis, or Thomas Roane, or their heirs, etc. shall pay to sd. Birt, the full amount of the three Bonds given by the sd. Curtis to the sd. Birt with the sd. Charles Curtis and Thomas Roane as Securities; one of the Bonds payable 1 Jan 1791, no others of the Bonds payable on 1 Jan 1792, the other Bond payable 1 Jan 1793, then this Indenture and conveyance therein contained to be void. Wits.: Thos. Healy, Jas. Healy, Thos. Healy, Junr. Signed: Wm. Curtis. Ackn.: 28 Jun 1790 - The Deed was recorded at Middlesex Co. Court House, Urbanna – Will Churchill.

Pg 188. 28 Oct 1789. I, William Gest, of Middlesex Co., VA, for £37, paid to me by Overton Cosby, **has sold to sd. Cosby the following Slaves, to wit – Peter, Sarah, & her children Sylva and Tom and to hold sd. Slaves and their future increase unto the sd. Cosby forever.** And, I , William Gest for myself do warrant and defend the Title to the sd. Slaves against any claim. Wits.: Peter Kemp, Junr., Thomas Bray. Signed: William Gest. And, WHEREAS, the absd. William Gest is at present in custody on a Writ at the suit of Overton Cosby and James Gregorie, surviving partners of James Mills & Co., the absd. Bill of Sale and conveyance is intended only to secure the payment of the debt and damages that shall be awarded by the Judgment of the County Court of Middlesex, whenever the suit shall be determined as witness my hand this date. Wits.: Peter Kemp, Junr., Thomas Bray. Signed: Overton Cosby. Ackn.: 28 Jun 1790 - The Bill of Sale was recorded at Middlesex Co. Court House, Urbanna – Will Churchill.

Pg 189. 22 Feb 1790. Ralph Wormeley, Junr., of Middlesex Co., VA, and Eleanor, his wife, sell to James Healy, of the afsd. place, for £60, for a parcel of land being by survey 30 a.; bnd. by lands of Littleton Watson & Ralph Wormeley, Junr., Esqrs., beg. at a point on the s. side of the main road in John South's line, then n. several courses to a point in Littleton Watson's line, and then along an old line of trees along a courses to the beg. Wits.: Francis Corbin,

Ralph Wormeley, Shelton [Skelton?] Murray. Signed: Ralph Wormeley, Eleanor Wormeley. Ackn.: 28 Jun 1790 - The Deed was recorded at Middlesex Co. Court House, Urbanna – Will Churchill.

Pg 190/ 28 Jun 1790. John Healy of Middlesex Co, VA, and Jane, his wife, sell to Benjamin Seward, of the afsd. place, for £15, for a piece of land in the afsd. place, beg. at a point cornering on the land of Henry Shepard and then joining the land of John Healy, being part of the tr. that he bot. from Daniel Dejarnet and cornering on land of Francis Oliver and then some courses to the land of Benjamin Seward and then to the beg., being 15 a. Wits.: None. Signed; Jno. Healy, Jeane Healy. Ackn.: 28 Jun 1790 - The Deed was recorded at Middlesex Co. Court House, Urbanna – Will Churchill.

Pg. 192. 24 May 1790. Thomas Crittenden and Jane, his wife, of the town of Urbanna, Parish of Christ Church, Middlesex Co., VA, sell to Leven Gale, Esqr., of the Parish of Somerset, Somerset Co., MD, for £75, for seven (7) lots of land in the Town of Urbanna afsd., and known on the plat map of the town as lots #13, 14, 15, 16, 18, 19, and 20, and sd. Gale to pay the £75 bef. 27 May 1792 with lawful interest from this date. Wits.: S. H. Henry, Thomas Muse, George Dame, William Blake. Signed: Thos. Crittenden, Jeane Crittenden. Ackn.: 28 Jun 1790 - The Deed was recorded at Middlesex Co. Court House, Urbanna – Will Churchill.

Pg 194. 28 Jun 1790. Thomas Crittenden and Jane, his wife, of Middlesex Co., VA, sell to Benjamin Seward, of the afsd. place, for £43, 11 shillings, for a parcel of land form. belonging to Nelson Daniel and then to a corner of Francis Oliver, and then a straight course joining the land of Francis Oliver and then to a corner of sd. Oliver and Benjamin Seward, and then s. to joining land of sd. Seward and then to land late of John George, and then to a corner of the sd. John George and Nelson Daniel and then to Daniels land and to the beg., being 33.5 a. Wits.: None. Signed: Thos. Crittenden, Janey Crittenden. Ackn.: 28 Jun 1790 - The Deed was recorded at Middlesex Co. Court House, Urbanna – Will Churchill.

Pg 196. 10 Jul 1790. Thomas Iverson, of Middlesex Co., VA, of the one part, and William Curtis, of the afsd. place, of the other part. WITNESSETH, that for £37, wch. he the afsd. Iverson is justly indebted to the afsd. Curtis and wants to secure and pay him, and for the further sum of 5 shillings to the sd. Iverson paid by the sd. Curtis, does hereby discharge the sd. Curtis, and he **the sd. Iverson has granted and sold to the sd. Curtis, one Negro Fellow named Patrick, also a Negro Boy named Harry, to have and to hold the Negroes and other premises forever,** IN TRUST, and shall after 10 Jul 1791 sell the sd. Negroes and premises and the money from same be used to pay the debt of £37 with interest from 10 Jul 1790. Wits.: P. Kemp. Junr., W. Segar, Wilkinson Barzey.

Signed: Thomas Iverson. Ackn.: 26 Jul 1790 - The Deed of Trust was recorded at Middlesex Co. Court House, Urbanna – Will Churchill.

Pg 197. 24 May 1790. Leven Gale, Esqr., of the Parish of Somerset, Somerset Co., MD, sells to Thomas Crittenden, of the Parish of Christ Church, Middlesex Co., VA, for £75, for a parcels o f land, or lots, in the town of Urbanna, Middlesex Co., VA, as described in the plat of the sd. town and numbered as Lots 13,14,15,16,18, 19, and 20, including sd. Gale's Rights to the sd. lots known on the plat of the town as #24 forever, NEVER THE LESS saving and reserving unto sd. Leven Gale and the heirs of his body lawfully begotten, the Right of the family burying place, to uses the same for the purpose of burial or to enclose the same in respect to the memory of the deceased their interred, free & unmolested of & by the sd. Crittenden and his heirs and assigns forever. Wits.: S. H. Henry, Thomas Muse, George Dame, William Blake. Signed: Liven Gale. Ackn.: 26 Jul 1790 - The Deed was recorded at Middlesex Co. Court House, Urbanna – Will Churchill.

Pg 200. 28 May 1790. Mary Stevens, of Middlesex Co., VA, sells to Alexander Bristow, of the afsd. place, for £16, 18 shillings, for a certain piece of land in the afsd. Co., beg. at the fork road on Mary Stevens' Land and leading down the Creek road to Benjamin William's line and then along same to James Lee's line and then along same to Reuben Lee's line and then along same until it makes 26 a. Wits.: James Lee, Plummer Thurston, George Lee. Signed: Mary Stevens. Ackn.: 26 Jul 1790 - The Deed was recorded at Middlesex Co. Court House, Urbanna – Will Churchill.

Pg 201. 24 Dec 1790. Francis Corbin, of Middlesex Co., VA, sells to Leven Gale, of Somerset Co., MD, for £763, 15 shillings, for a tr. of landing the afsd. place, betw. the fork of a creek called Grangs Creek, being 750 a. Wits.; Overton Cosby, Jno. Segar, Wilson Lumpkin, Peter Kemp, Junr., P. Kemp, Edward Ware. Signed: Francis Corbin. Ackn.: 27 Dec 1790 - The Deed of Mortgage was recorded at Middlesex Co. Court House, Urbanna – Will Churchill.

Pg 203. 11 Nov 1790. I, Joshua Hughes, of Louisa Co., VA, has appointed Charles Yancey, Jr., of the afsd. Co., to be his lawful attorney to act and transact all his business respecting the proportion of Daniel Stringer's Estate, dec'd, of Middlesex Co. VA, wch. I am entitled to as being a legatee of sd. Estate. Wits.: Isaac Carleton, Charles Daniel, John Dicken, Junr. Signed: Joshua Hughes. Ackn.: 27 Dec 1790 - The Power of Attorney was recorded at Middlesex Co. Court House, Urbanna – Will Churchill.

Pg 204. 27 Dec 1790. William Steptoe, Gent., and Elizabeth, his wife, of Middlesex Co., VA, sell to Hudson Muse, Naval Officer, of the other part, for 32 sheep paid by the sd. Muse, for a lot of land in the town of Urbanna, being lot

22, wch. was form. the property of Christopher Robinson, Esqr. dec'd, and became the sd. Steptoe's upon his intermarriage with the sd. Elizabeth, his wife, and being all the land that the sd. William Steptoe and Elizabeth, his wife, hold in the town of Urbanna. Wits.: Will Churchill, Thomas Segar, Thos. Roane. Signed: Will. Steptoe, Eliza. Steptoe. 27 Dec 1790 – Thomas Segar and Thomas Roane examined Elizabeth Steptoe. Ackn.: 28 Dec 1790 - The Deed was recorded at Middlesex Co. Court House, Urbanna – Will Churchill.

Pg 206. 25 Aug 1790. John Woodley, of Middlesex Co., VA, of one part and Robert Spratt, of the other part. WITNESSETH, that for £4, 10 shillings, wch. the sd. Woodley is indebted to the sd. Spratt and desires to secure and to pay him, and in further consideration of 5 shillings to sd. Woodley paid by sd. Spratt, doth hereby sell to Robert Spratt forever, 1 feather bed, 1 black walnut table, 1 iron pot, 1 pair of tongs, 1 iron ladle, 7 pewter plates, and 1 dish, 1 black walnut chest, 1 bedstead & bed cord[?], 1 pine chest, 4 chairs, 5 hogs, 1 washing tub, 2 pails, 2 axes, and all the other items pertaining to the premises. AND, to hold all these items and other premises to the proper use of sd. Spratt, UPON TRUST, and after 1 Jan 1791 to sell these items in order to settle the debt of £4, 10 shillings, with lawful interest from 1 Feb 1790. Wits.: Staige Davis, Peter Kemp. Signed: John Woodley, made his mark. Ackn.: 28 Dec 1790 - The Deed of Trust was recorded at Middlesex Co. Court House, Urbanna – Will Churchill.

Pg 208. 28 Jun 1790. John George, and Suckey, his wife, of King & Queen Co., VA, sell to William Lumpkin, of Middlesex Co., VA, for £160, for a tr. of land, being 129.5 a., in Middlesex Co. afsd., agreeable to a survey by Isaac Carlton, the Co. Surveyor, done on 2 Jul 1789, beg. at a point at the mouth of Cordwell's Spring branch and corner of Mary Shepherd, and then to a corner of George Bird[?], and then several courses to the main run of Dragon Swamp and to a corner of Isaac Diggs, and then up the run to a corner of John Seward, and then several courses to Shepherd's corner and then down the sd. run to the beg. AND, ALSO on other tr. in the afsd. Co., being 6 a. bnd by a survey made by sd. Carlton in 1789, beg. at a corner of Lunsford Daniel and then to another of his corners, and then several courses to a corner of Benjamin Seward and John Seward, and then to the beg. The plats of both surveys being hereunto annexed. Wits.: P. Kemp, Jas. Ross, B. Kidd, Junr. Signed: John George, Junr., Susanna George. Ackn.: 27 Dec 1790 - The Deed was recorded at Middlesex Co. Court House, Urbanna – Will Churchill.

Pg 210. 15 Jul 1790. Philip Ludwell Grymes, Esqr., of the Parish of Christ Church, Middlesex Co., VA, and Judith, his wife, of the one part and Richard Davis, of the afsd. place, of the other part. WHEREAS, Philip Grymes, Esqr., dec'd, father of the sd. Philip Ludwell Grymes, did in his lifetime sell unto the sd. Richard Davis, a tr. of land in afsd. place, being 300 a. BUT, bef. his father executed the deed for same, he departed this life. NOW THIS INDENTURE, Philip Ludwell Grymes for £176 paid to the Executors of the sd. Philip Grymes, dec'd, sells by these Presents unto the sd. Richard Davis and assigns the tr. of land that was greed to be conveyed to the sd. Davis, being 300 a., beg. at an Antient Corner at the fork of Barbeque Creek opposite to store point, then up sd. creek to a corner commonly called Sir Henry Chishley's Corner at the head of sd. creek and then to sd. Barbeque Creek and then to Armistead's land and running the courses of the late survey, with all Rights of the sd. Philip Ludwell Grymes and Judith, his wife. Wits.: William Stiff, John Robinson, Ralph Wormeley, Wm. Wood. Signed: Philip L. Grymes, Judith Grymes. Ackn.: 24 Jan 1791 - The Deed was recorded at Middlesex Co. Court House, Urbanna – Will Churchill.

Pg 212. 1 Jul 1789. I, Thomas Iverson, of Middlesex Co., VA, for £10, 5 shillings, 6 pence, due and owing by me unto William Churchill, of the afsd. place, and also for 5 shillings paid to me by sd. Churchill, have herby granted and sold unto sd. Churchill – **4 Negro slaves, to wit: Glasgow, James, Tom and Harry,** and also 2 horses by the names of Damon and Mark Anthony. Wits.: James Bradfut [Bradford?]. Signed: Thomas Iverson. Ackn.: 28 Feb 1791 - The Bill of Sale was recorded at Middlesex Co. Court House, Urbanna – Will Churchill.

Pg 213. 13 Apr 1791. Gideon Mims, of Goochland Co., VA, of the one part, and Iron Monger Major, of Middlesex Co., VA, for in consideration of annual rent of £7, 10 shillings, to be paid by Iron Monger Major to sd. Mims on 1 Jan 1791 and on 1 Jan in every succeeding year, hath leased, demised, and farm letten unto sd. Major for the term and during the life of Polly Mims, the wife of Jesee Mims, for all that plantation of land wch. the sd. Polly now holds in Middlesex Co. afsd., as the widow and relict of John Miller, dec'd, being 365 a., for and during the life of the sd. Polly, and the sd. Iron Monger Major is to keep the dwelling house in repair and the sd. Gideon Mims will warrant the sd. land afsd to the sd. Iron Monger Major. Wits.: Will Churchill, Dudley Vaughan, Robert Dudley, William [N/V.?] Stiff. Signed: Gideon Mims, Ire Monger Major. Ackn.: 25 Apr 1791 - The Deed of Lease was recorded at Middlesex Co. Court House, Urbanna – Will Churchill.

Pg 214. 18 Feb 1791. Chowning Kidd and Cathren, his wife, of Middlesex Co., VA, sells to Alexander Bristow, of the afsd. place, for the just quantity of 10,000 pounds of crop tobacco, sells unto sd. Bristow, a parcel of land in the afsd. place, in the fork of Francis Corbin's Mill bnd. by the lands of Henry Chowning and Francis Corbin, being 60 a. Wits.: James Lee, Wm. Jessee, George Bray. Signed: Chowning Kidd and Cathren Kidd, both made their marks. Ackn.: 25 Apr 1791 - The Deed was recorded at Middlesex Co. Court House, Urbanna – Will Churchill.

Pg 215. 16 Feb 1789. In obedience of an Order of the worshipful Court of Middlesex, we the subscribers whose names is hereto subscribed have allotted and laid off to Dorothy Miller, late widow of John Berry, dec'd, 65 a. of land for the Dower in the sd. lands called Store Point, bnd. agreeable to a plot hereto annexed reference thereto being had may more fully appear. Signed: John Wake, Thos. Hunton, John Sutton, Dudley Vaughan. [A hand drawn map is beneath the above wch. shows the land area of wch. has "Orphans Part", 130 a., and 65 a., with ponds and creeks.]

Beneath the above drawing is the following: 16 Feb 1789 - In obedience of an Order of the worshipful Court of Middlesex, dated 26 Jan 1789, I went in Company with John Wake, Thomas Hunton, John Sutton and Dudley Vaughan, and agreeable to their direction Surveyed the land of John Berry, late husband, of Dorothy Miller, and laid off her Thirds of the same, it being the land known by the name of Store Point and bnd. as follows: Beg. at a point on the n.w. side of a small creek that empties into a creek betw. Store Point & William Jackson's – namely opposite the sd. Jackson's House, and then up the sd. Creek and across the narrowest of Store Point, 132 poles to Pranketank[?] from there down Pranketank[?] 120.5 poles to a small pine, the dividing line from then around Store point to the beg. Signed: Isaac Carlton, S. Msx.

Middlesex Co. – 26 Jan 1789 - Ordered that John Wake, Thomas Hunton, John Sutton and Dudley Vaughan, or any three of them, lay off to Dorothy Miller, her dower, in the lands of John Berry, her late husband, and make their report to the next Court. Copy last – Will Churchill. Ackn.: 26 Jan 1790 – This allotment for Dorothy Miller's Dower in the lands of John Berry, her late husband, returned and Ordered to be recorded – Will Churchill.

Pg 216. 23 Nov 1789. Know ye, that James Ross, Edmund Berkeley and Overton Cosby are held and firmly bound unto Beverly Randolph, Gov. of VA, for £1,000. The Condition of the above is that James Ross is appointed Sheriff of the County and that he truly perform his prescribed duties of his office. Wits.: None. Signed: Jas. Ross, Edmd. Berkeley and Overton Cosby. Ackn.: 23 Nov 1789 - The Bond was recorded at Middlesex Co. Court House, Urbanna – Will Churchill.

Pg 216. 23 Nov 1789. Know ye, that James Ross, Edmund Berkeley, and Overton Cosby, are held and firmly bound unto Jaquilan Ambler, Treasurer of VA, for £10,000. The Condition of the above is that James Ross faithfully collect and account for all taxes of Middlesex Co. and that he truly perform his prescribed duties of his office. Wits.: None. Signed: Jas. Ross, Edmd. Berkeley and Overton Cosby. Ackn.: 23 Nov 1789 - The Bond was recorded at Middlesex Co. Court House, Urbanna – Will Churchill.

Pg 217. 22 Jun 1789. Henry Chowning and Thomas Healy are firmly bound unto James Wood, Lt. Gov. of VA, for the time being for £1,000. The Condition of the obligation is that Henry Chowning is appointed Inspector of tobacco at the public warehouse and that he faithfully discharge the duties of his office. Wits.: None. Signed: Henry Chowning, Thos. Healy. Ackn.: 22 Jun 1789 - The Bond was recorded at Middlesex Co. Court House, Urbanna – Will Churchill.

Pg 217. 8 Jun 1789. James Quarles and Mary, his wife, [no location] sells to John Jackson, of Middlesex Co., VA, for £105, 5 shillings, for a tr. of land on Rapahannock River, in the Parish of Christ Church, Middlesex Co., VA, and commonly called by the name of Pine Top, being 105.25 a., according to a survey by Isaac Carlton, on 6th of this instant, beg. at a point on the s. side of the mouth of a cove of Little Oyster Creek, then crossing the cove and running up the afsd. River, then up to a line cornering to John Batchelder, then several courses to a corner of Wake and Churchill, and then a course to John Jackson, and then a courses back to the beg. Wits.; Thos. Hanson[?], made his mark, William Jackson, James Batchelder, Benja. Hackney, William Hill. Signed: James Quarles, Mary Quarles. 29 Jun 1789 – James Hill and Isaac Quarles examined Mary Quarles. Ackn.: 27 Oct 1789 - The Deed was certified at Middlesex Co. Court House, Urbanna – Will Churchill.

THE END

****

31, 35, 40, 47, 50, 51, 52, 53, 54,
55, 61, 62, 69, 93; William, 108,
109
BLAKEY, Churchill, 76; Ann, 76,
77; Churchill, 17, 28, 38, 52, 77,
82, 106
BOSS, John, 34, 40, 54, 56, 57, 87;
Thomas, 81; William, 54
BOSWELL, Macham, 102
BOUGHTON, John, 49
BOWDEN, Sally, 76; William, 20,
76; Wm., 96, 100, 104
BOWDEN[?], William, Senr., 13
BOXLEY, William, 36
BOYD, James, 30
BRADFORT, James, 73
BRADFUT[BRADFORD?], James,
111
BRAXTON, Carter, 6, 32, 61
BRAY, George, 111; Peter, 90, 99;
Richard, 29, 40; Thomas, 99,
107
BREAM, John, 46; John, dec'd, 46
BRISTOW, Alexander, 32, 38, 109,
111; Alexd., 89; Bartholomew, 30,
31, 40, 64, 103; Benjamin, 12, 27,
34, 57, 103; Edward, dec'd, 11;
Fanny, 103, 104; James, 103;
Josiah, 93, 99, 103, 104; Lenard,
96; Molley, 103; Nancy, 103;
Rich., 96; Richard, 17; Richd., 99;
William, 5, 25, 30, 31, 32, 33, 38,
40; William, Junr., 18
BROOK, Thomas, 86; William, 13
BROOKING, John, 66
BROOKS, Edward, 2, 9, 29, 40; John,
20, 43, 47, 98, 106; Samuel, 12,
47, 67; Thomas, 1, 17, 76, 77;
William, 1, 8, 17
BROOKS[?], Thomas, 98
BROWN, Wm., 90
BRUMMELL, [FNU], 91; Wm.
Hudgin, 79
BRUMMIL, [FNU], 85

BRUMMILL, William Hudgin, 79
BURK, Thomas, 70
BURN, Dennis, 31
BURNELL, John, London Mayor, 80
BURNHAM, [FNU], 81
BURT, Harwood, 104
BURTON, Robert, 71
BURWELL, Lewis, dec'd, 33
BUSH, George, 35, 50, 55; Thomas,
81

C

CALAHAM, William, 77
CAMPBELL, James, 48
CANADY, Ambrose, dec'd, 74
CARDWELL, Richard, 29, 40
CARDWELL'S SPRING BRANCH,
92
CARLETON, Isaac, 85, 93, 109
CARLETON[?], Isaac, 92
CARLTON, Isaac, 22, 94, 100, 113;
Isaac, County Surveyor, 110;
Isaac, Surveyor, 84, 112
CARPENTER, Nathaniel, 26
CARTER, [Cenejin?], 77; Cinyon,
77; John, 70; Joseph, 87; Martha,
70
CHISHLEY, Henry, Sir, 111
CHOWNING, [FNU], 93; Fanny,
101; Henry, 14, 15, 38, 39, 43,
47, 50, 51, 52, 53, 54, 55, 61,
62, 90, 94, 111, 112, 113; John,
orphan, 1; Robert, 64, 97, 101,
106; Samuel, 5, 29, 30, 31, 60;
Sarah, 14, 15; Thomas, 25, 67;
Thomas, dec'd, 14, 15; William,
15, 24, 94
CHRIST CHURCH PARISH, 11
CHRISTIAN SOCIETY OF
BAPTISTS, 65
CHURCHHILL, William, 63
CHURCHILL, [FNU], 91; Armistead,
87; Armistead, Esqr., 80; Benja.,
72, 73; Benjamin, 42, 72; Eliza,

Hannah, 19; James, 98; Jas.[?], 77; Jno., 77; John, 12, 15, 24, 32, 49, 67, 74, 76, 77, 85, 86, 98, 106; John, dec'd, 5, 60, 74; Lunsford, 78, 92, 93, 94, 95, 96, 101, 105, 110; Lydia, 92, 93, 96, 101; Lucy, 103; Mary, 78, 92, 94; Milly, 103; Molley, 22; N., 94, 96, 97; N.[?], 92, 94; Nelson, 2, 12, 15, 32, 34, 36, 42, 65, 78, 95, 101, 105, 108; Overton, 13, 76, 86, 89; Robert, 11, 28, 38, 46, 56, 74, 75, 104; Robert, dec'd, 5, 28, 61, 62; Robert, Junr., 74; Samuel, 46, 50, 51; Susanna, 9, 14, 78, 85, 93, 94; Susanna G., 92, 94; Susanna, widow, 78; William, dec'd, 19, 78; William, Dec'd, 93
DANIEL'S SPRING BRANCH, 91
DANIELS, Millie, Mrs., 86; Susanna, 2
DAVIES, John, 37
DAVIS, Andrew, 13, 33, 45, 49, 69, 81, 106; Elizabeth, 13, 106; Geo., 64, 69; Geo. B., 83, 84, 85, 89, 106; George, 27, 46, 74, 85; George B., 87; George, dec'd, 56; Richard, 72, 105, 110, 111; Sarah, 106; Staige, 69, 74, 83, 84, 87, 88, 89, 95, 96, 103, 104, 105, 110; William, 105
DAVIS[?], William, 47; Williamson, 86
DE SEGOUGNE, Julie, 100; Louis, 100
DEAGLE, Benjamin, 33
DEAN, John, 52, 65; William, 19
DEGGES, Isaac, 56, 58
DEJARNAT, Daniel, 14
DEJARNATT, Daniel, 17, 18, 30, 42, 43, 56, 57, 68, 73, 85; Daniel[?], 22; Susannah, 73
DEJARNET, Daniel, 108
DEJARNETT, [FNU], 91; Daniel,

1, 2, 74; Elisabeth, 85
DENESON, Jonathan, 62
DENISON, Jane, 93; Jonathan, 47, 50, 51, 52, 53, 54, 55, 61, 64, 78, 90; Joseph Lewis, 90; William, 90
DENNISON, Jonathan, 19, 21, 36
DICKEN, John, Junr., 109
DIDLAKE, Edward, 2, 29, 56, 57
DIGGS, Isaac, 44, 92, 110
DILLARD, Elizabeth, 14; George, 28, 47, 68, 70, 94; John, dec'd, 68; Mary, 93
DILLARD'S ORDINARY, 17
DILLIARD, George, 92, 93; Mary, 92
DOR_____[?], Mary, 2
DRUMMOND, Samuel, 45
DUDLEY, Ann, 2, 10, 14; Charles, 14, 79, 81, 95, 102; Harry, 70; Jane, 25; Mary, 7; Nancy, 47, 79; Robert, 78, 111; Sarah, 68; William, 3, 59, 93
DULUS[?], Charles, 92
DUNLEVY, George, 52; James, 16, 17, 18, 19, 20, 70, 87, 89; John, 2; William, 16
DUNN, Agrippa, 15, 22, 36, 47, 86; Aquippa, 17

E

EARNEST[?], Samuel, 40
EDGAR, Anna Maria, 80, 97; Thomas, 97; Thomas, ship carpenter, 80
EDMONDSON, Philip, 56
EDWARDS, Charles, 16, 27, 47, 57, 70; Thomas, 2, 55
ELIOTT'S WAREHOUSE, 103
ELLIOT, Charles, 36; Elizabeth, dec'd, 41; Matthew, 17, 22, 36; William, 3, 17, 21, 35, 36, 41, 44
ELLIOTT, Elizabeth, 72; Elizabeth, dec'd, 71; Matthew, 72; William,

58, 59, 71, 72; Wm., 72, 83
EMBERSON, Nancy, 99
ERNEST, Samuel, 36
EYRE, Jonathan, 52, 56

F

FALKNER, Evey, 69; Thoms, 69
FAULKNER, James, orphan, 18;
  John, 18
FEARN[?], Meacham, 33
FERGUSON, Robert, 70
FITZHUGH, George, 103
FLEET, Baylor, 70; Edwin, 3, 59, 93;
  Henry, 3, 59; John, 93; William, 3,
  59, 70, 93; Wm., 70
FLEMING, Charles, 17, 22, 36
FORMAN, George, 32
FOWLERS, George, 7, 46, 48, 49, 61;
  John, 7, 46, 48, 49, 61
FRANCIS CORBIN'S MILL, 111
FRASER, Simon, 48, 49, 50, 71
FURNELL, George, 31

G

GAINS, Thomas, 30, 58
GALE, Leven, 98; Leven, Esqr., 108,
  109; Levin, 98; Liven, 109
GARDNER, Ann, 86; Anthony, 100;
  George, 64; Jack, 55, 56; John, 29
GARLAND, Christopher, 86; David,
  89, 103
GAYLE, Joseph, 6, 13, 35
GEORGE, [FNU], 91; Agathy, 74; H.,
  93; James, 74; Jhn, Junr., 74; John,
  15, 16, 17, 18, 19, 20, 21, 23, 25,
  26, 27, 28, 36, 38, 39, 40, 41,42,
  80, 83, 86, 92, 94, 95, 97, 101,108,
  110; John, Junr., 2, 10, 43, 56, 65,
  68, 74, 79, 80, 96, 104, 110; John,
  Senr., 106; Leonard, 104, 105;
  Meacham, 66, 79, 92, 93; Suckey,
  110; Susanna, 74, 110; W., 67, 80,
  82, 86, 90, 91, 97, 102, 104, 105;
  William, 11, 33, 36, 43, 44, 47,

50, 51, 52, 53, 54, 55, 61, 62, 86,
  104
GEST, Mary, 66, 92; William, 3, 48,
  58, 59, 66, 92, 107
GIBSON, Wm., 97
GILL, Hannah, 33
GOOD, John, 64
GOOSLEY, William, 10, 33
GORDON, John, 87; Lucy, 87
GOSLER, Jon Craine, 16
GRAHAM, W., 67
GRAY'S POINT, 102
GREEN, George, 4, 33, 36, 59;
  Robert, 3
GREENWOOD, Josiah, 49; Samuel,
  19; Sibel, 19
GREGORIE, Ja., 84; James, 5, 23,
  24, 32, 60, 74, 83, 94, 95, 96,
  107
GREGORY, Ja., 87; James, 87
GROOM, John, 86; Robert, 86, 90;
  Thomas, 90
GROOM[?], John, 17
GROOME, John, 18
GRYMES, Charles, 2, 9, 10, 27,
  32, 33, 35, 37, 38, 43, 44;
  Charles, Esqr., 103; Jane, 27;
  John R., 88; John Randolph,
  88; John Randolph, Esqr., 70,
  71; Judith, 110, 111; Philip L.,
  69, 96; Philip Ludwell, 5, 7, 14,
  18, 26, 27, 33, 39, 49, 81, 111;
  Philip Ludwell, Esqr., 97, 110;
  Philip Ludwill, 88; Philip, dec'd,
  110; Philip, Esqr., 62
GULLEY, Philip, 42

H

HACKNEY, Benja., 113; Benjamin,
  32, 37, 44, 56, 72, 105; Elizabeth,
  3, 59; Sara, 66; Sarah, 66;
  William, 2, 3, 16, 52, 59, 66, 95,
  96, 105; Wm., 105
HADDEN, Mary, dec'd, 58

98; Negro, Mary[?], 101; Negro, Menerva, 89; Negro, Michael, 98; Negro, Michaell[?], 98; Negro, Mill, 101; Negro, Milly[?], 85; Negro, Moll[?], 101; Negro, Nancy, 98; Negro, Nanny, 92, 95, 98; Negro, Nanny and/or Brandy Still, 97; Negro, Narry, 95; Negro, Nathaniel, 104; Negro, Old Betty, 98; Negro, Old Dick, 98; Negro, Peg, 88; Negro, Pene, 88; Negro, Peter, 107; Negro, Phebey, 98; Negro, Philis, 96; Negro, Phill, 96; Negro, Philles, 88; Negro, Polly, 89; Negro, Pompey, 95; Negro, Ralph, 95; Negro, Robin, 88, 95, 98; Negro, Rose, 88; Negro, Sally, 88, 95, 96; Negro, Samuel, 98; Negro, Sarah, 101; Negro, Sarah, and her children, Sylva & Tom, 107; Negro, Scipia[?], 88; Negro, Somerset, 98; Negro, Steptow, 98; Negro, Subey[?], 88; Negro, Sukey, 98; Negro, Sylva, dau. of Sarah, 107; Negro, Tangion, 88; Negro, Toby, 98; Negro, Tom, 88, 111; Negro, Tom, son of Sarah, 107; Negro, Venisel[?], 88; Negro, Venus, 88; Negro, Will, 98; Negroe Cassius, 5; Negro Daphny, 1; Negro Frank, 5; Negro Harry, 5; Negro Rachel, 5; Negro Sarah, 1; Negro, Nelson, 12; Negro, Phil, 84; Negro, Sally, 84; Negro, Sam, 84; Negro, Sarah, 12; Negro, Sinah, Negro woman, 42; Negro, Tom, 12; Negro, Vaughan, 84
SLAVES, Un-named, 26
SMITH, Adam Charles, 36, Amistead, 102; Augustine, 7, 33, 49, 61; Augustine, dec'd, 4, 65; Augustine, Estate of, 89; Fanny, 102; Jacob, of Henrico Co., 41;

John, 33, 36, 44, 49, 99; Major, 66; Maurice, 11, 12, 26, 27, 43, 44, 46, 57, 66, 67, 83, 90, 96, 99; Maurice, Coll., 102; Thomas, 70
SOLE, John, 2, 8, 10, 17, 21
SOLES, John, 12
SOUTH, John, 103
SOUTHERN, Avy, 64; George, 64
SPENCER, Edward, 3, 59; Thomas, 3
SPOTSWOOD, Elizabeth, 89; Hugh, 49
SPRATT, Robert, 11, 14, 23, 26, 37, 39, 50, 57, 87, 89, 110; Robert, Doctor, 91, 92; Robert, Esqr., 79; Robert, Physician, 69
STAMPER, Robert, 1, 8, 24, 26, 27, 82
STANDARD, Anna, 79, 80; Geo., 73, 79, 80; George, 79, 80
STANDARD[STANARD?], Ann, 72; Anna, 73; George, 72
STAPLES, William, 39
STEPTOE, [FNU], 86; Elizabeth, 109; Will, 100; William, 14, 82, 92, 109; Wm., 84
STEVENS, Mary, 109
STIFF, James, 14, 69, 72, 73; Jas., 69; Thomas, 47; William, 19, 52, 55, 72, 73, 82, 83, 94, 95, 111; William [N/V?], 111; William, Major, 102
STREET, Henry, 8, 63; Richard, 45, 63, 86
STRINGER, Caroline, 101; Daniel, 17, 35, 50, 92, 97, 106; Daniel, dec'd, 109; Daniel, Junr., 97, 101; Daniel, Senr., 96, 97; Daniel, the Elder, 101; Sarah, 106; William, 96, 97, 101
STRINGER[?], Daniel, 47
STUART, Charles, 32
STUBBS, Francis, 10
STURMAN, Elliot, 19, 21; Elliott, 100, 103; Mary, 100

Heritage Books by Richard S. Hutchinson:

Abstracts from the Land Records of Dorchester County, Maryland, 1719–1726

Abstracts of the Council of Safety Minutes State of New Jersey, 1777–1778

Abstracts of the Deaths and Marriages in the Hightstown Gazette *[New Jersey], 18 April 1861–28 December 1871*

Abstracts of the Deaths and Marriages in the Hightstown Gazette *[New Jersey], 4 January 1872–27 December 1877*

Abstracts of the Deaths and Marriages in the Hightstown Gazette *[New Jersey], 3 January 1878–29 December 1881*

Abstracts of the Deaths and Marriages in the Hightstown Gazette *[New Jersey], 5 January 1882–31 December 1885*

Abstracts of the Deaths and Marriages in the Hightstown Gazette *[New Jersey], 7 January 1886–26 December 1889*

Burlington County, New Jersey, Deed Abstracts: Books A, B and C

East New Jersey Land Records, 1702–1717 (Books H, I and "Little K")

East New Jersey Land Records, 1715–1722

East New Jersey Land Records, 1719–1727 (Books C-2 and D-2)

East New Jersey Land Records, 1727–1736/7

East New Jersey Land Records, 1737–1747

East New Jersey Land Records, 1747–1757

East New Jersey Land Records, 1757–1763

East New Jersey Land Records, 1763–1766

East New Jersey Land Records, 1766–1772

East New Jersey Land Records, 1772–1791

Lancaster County, Virginia Abstract of Wills, Administrations, Deeds, Inventories, Etc. 1736–1742
Tawny Waske and Richard S. Hutchinson

Lancaster County, Virginia Abstracts of Order Book 8 (Part 1), 1728–1737

Lancaster County, Virginia Abstracts of Order Book 8 (Part 2), May 1737–March 1743

Lancaster County, Virginia Deeds, 1714–1728

Lancaster County, Virginia: Abstracts of Wills, Administrations, Deeds, Inventories, Etc.: Book #12, 1726–1735

Lancaster County, Virginia: Abstracts of Wills, Administrations, Deeds, Inventories, Etc.: Book #14, 1743–1750

www.ingramcontent.com/pod-product-compliance
Lightning Source LLC
Chambersburg PA
CBHW071133280326
41935CB00010B/1212

* 9 7 8 1 6 8 0 3 4 4 8 6 8 *